WHAT A WORLD 3
LISTENING

P9-BJB-234

Amazing Stories
from Around the Globe

Milada Broukal

PEARSON
Longman

What a World Listening 3: Amazing Stories from Around the Globe

Copyright © 2011 by Pearson Education, Inc.
All rights reserved. No part of this publication may be reproduced, stored in a retrieval system, or transmitted in any form or by any means, electronic, mechanical, photocopying, recording, or otherwise, without the prior permission of the publisher.

Pearson Education, 10 Bank Street, White Plains, NY 10606 USA

Staff credits: The people who made up the **What a World Listening 3** team, representing editorial, production, design, and manufacturing, are Pietro Alongi, Rhea Banker, John Brezinsky, Aerin Csigay, Gina DiLillo, Nancy Flaggman, Oliva Fernandez, Lisa Ghiozzi, Jaime Lieber, Amy McCormick, Linda Moser, Jennifer Stem, Leigh Stolle, and Patricia Wosczyk.
Cover and text design: Patricia Wosczyk
Text composition: ElectraGraphics, Inc.
Text font: Minion
Photo Credits: Cover photo: Tom Till/Getty Images; Page 1 Shutterstock.com; 4 (left) Shutterstock.com, (right) Shutterstock.com; 9 Shutterstock.com; 12 (left) Shutterstock.com, (right) Shutterstock.com; 17 Shutterstock.com; 20 (left) Dreamstime.com, (right) Shutterstock.com; 25 Ann Rayworth/Alamy; 28 (left) Photos.com, (right) Dreamstime.com; 33 Shutterstock.com; 36 (left) Shutterstock.com, (right) Shutterstock.com; 41 Pierre Vauthey/Corbis Sygma; 45 (left) AP Images/Alex Brandon, (right) Mitchell Gerber/Corbis; 49 Shutterstock.com; 52 (left) Shutterstock.com, (right) Shutterstock.com; 57 Dreamstime.com; 60 (left) Dreamstime.com, (right) Dreamstime.com; 69 Shutterstock.com; 72 (left) Shutterstock.com, (right) Shutterstock.com; 77 Shutterstock.com; 80 (left) Shutterstock.com, (right) Shutterstock.com; 85 Shutterstock.com; 88 (left) Shutterstock.com, (right) Shutterstock.com; 93 Shutterstock.com; 96 (left) Shutterstock.com, (right) Shutterstock.com; 101 Shutterstock.com; 104 (left) Shutterstock.com, (right) Shutterstock.com; 109 Shutterstock.com; 112 (left) Shutterstock.com, (right) Shutterstock.com; 118 Stan Wayman/Photo Researchers, Inc.; 121 (left) Shutterstock.com, (right) Shutterstock.com; 126 Andrew Brusso/Corbis; 130 (left) AP Images/Ben Margot, (right) AP Images/Marcio Jose Sanchez.

Library of Congress Cataloging-in-Publication Data

Broukal, Milada.
  What a world listening: amazing stories from around the globe / Milada Broukal.
      p. cm.—(What a world listening: amazing stories from around the globe series)
  Previously published as: What a world, 2004.
  ISBN 0-13-247389-5 (v. 1)—ISBN 0-13-247795-5 (v. 2)—ISBN 0-13-138200-4 (v. 3) 1. English language—Textbooks for foreign speakers. 2. Listening. I. Title
  PE1128.B717 2010
  428.2'4—dc21

                                                                    2010037494

ISBN-13: 978-0-13-138200-8
ISBN-10: 0-13-138200-4

PEARSON LONGMAN ON THE WEB

Pearsonlongman.com offers online resources for teachers and students. Access our Companion Websites, our online catalog, and our local offices around the world.

Visit us at **www.pearsonlongman.com**.

Printed in the United States of America
1 2 3 4 5 6 7 8 9 10–V011–19 18 17 16 15 14 13 12 11 10

CONTENTS

INTRODUCTION	vii		

UNIT	VOCABULARY	LANGUAGE FOCUS	PRONUNCIATION
1 **WHAT ARE SOME FAMOUS CASTLES AROUND THE WORLD?** PAGES **1–8**	*acquired • besides • design • exasperating • excursion • hired • impressive • publisher* *guest list • historic sites • made his fortune*	Tag Questions	Intonation for Tag Questions
2 **WHAT DO YOU KNOW ABOUT ANCIENT CIVILIZATIONS OF THE AMERICAS?** PAGES **9–16**	*anticipated • astonishing • captured • complex • conquering • massive • revealing • ruins* *above sea level • set off • settled in*	Participles as Adjectives	The Sound *beige* /ʒ/
3 **WHAT ARE SOME FAMOUS FESTIVALS AROUND THE WORLD?** PAGES **17–24**	*entire • fast • harvest • immortal • incense • proceeded • reunions • tucked* *dates back to • in observance of • long for*	Non-action Verbs	Silent Letters
4 **WHO ARE SOME FAMOUS LEGENDARY CHARACTERS?** PAGES **25–32**	*abused • corresponds • enforce • fugitive • infamous • manipulated • outlaw • tyranny* *based on • good-hearted • took over*	*used to* and *would* + Base Verb	The *s* Sound in *used to* and *use / used*
5 **WHAT ARE SOME FAMOUS TEMPLES AROUND THE WORLD?** PAGES **33–40**	*academics • deserted • enlightenment • pilgrimage • reliefs • replica • restore • shrine* *bound by • place of worship • put together*	Passive Voice	Sentence Intonation and Stress
6 **WHO ARE SOME FAMOUS FASHION DESIGNERS?** PAGES **41–48**	*bold • boutique • determined • freelance • garment • prestigious • trendsetter • will* *end up • flea market • paved the way*	Past Perfect	Linking *'d* in the Past Perfect Tense

UNIT	VOCABULARY	LANGUAGE FOCUS	PRONUNCIATION
7 HOW DO PEOPLE AROUND THE WORLD EAT? PAGES **49–56**	*belch • etiquette • inappropriate • indicate • offend • punctuality • slurp • utensils* *a crash course • fit in • make a good impression*	*so that, in order to*	The Sounds *sherry* /ʃ/ and *cherry* /tʃ/
8 HOW DO PEOPLE CELEBRATE A WEDDING? PAGES **57–64**	*affairs • consider • devotion • fidelity • gown • locals • reception • union* *familiar with • give their blessings • run across*	*may, might, could* for Possibility (Review); *maybe* or *may be*	*maybe* and *may be*
9 WHAT ARE SOME FAMOUS BURIAL TOMBS AROUND THE WORLD? PAGES **69–76**	*artifacts • currency • defend • excavations • legacy • recreate • ruthless • standardized* *concerns about • hit upon • life-size*	More Rules for the Article *the*	The Sounds *the* /ðə/ and *the* /ði/
10 WHAT ARE SOME FAMOUS VOLCANOES AROUND THE WORLD? PAGES **77–84**	*amateur • constantly • countless • current • emerged • erupted • intact • lava* *hot temper • put up with • takes up*	Unreal Conditional in the Past	Contraction of *have*
11 WHO ARE SOME FAMOUS PEOPLE FROM THE RENAISSANCE? PAGES **85–92**	*apprentice • contemplating • diverse • manuscripts • sketched • swore • theory • weapons* *a handful of • beyond a doubt • thought up*	*must (not) have / can't / could (not) have*	Shifting Stress on Suffixes
12 WHAT ARE SOME UNUSUAL SPORTS IN THE WORLD? PAGES **93–100**	*athletic • boulder • hilarious • leisurely • navigate • penalty • squash • stream* *adept at • depending on • figure out*	Gerund after Prepositions and Certain Expressions	The Letter *o*
13 WHAT IS OCEANIA? PAGES **101–108**	*characteristics • comprise • generations • genuine • pristine • resort • staple • upbringing* *get together • laid-back • scented with*	Future Time Clauses	Homophones

UNIT	VOCABULARY	LANGUAGE FOCUS	PRONUNCIATION
14 **WHAT ARE SOME SPICES OF THE WORLD?** PAGES **109–117**	*appreciate • block • curry • enhance • milder • novel • spoils • tolerate* *acquire a taste for • contribute to • make sense*	Verbs with Gerunds; Verbs with Infinitives; Verbs with Gerunds or Infinitives	Expressing Emotions with Intonation
15 **HOW DOES SCIENCE EXPLORE THE SEA TODAY?** PAGES **118–125**	*discharge • ecosystem • fluids • frigid • illuminate • thriving • vents • withstand* *forms of • lack of • spewed from*	Future Perfect and Future Perfect Progressive	The Schwa Sound: *was* /ə/
16 **WHO BROUGHT US THE WORLD WIDE WEB?** PAGES **126–133**	*access • advertisements • attention • diminish • modest • preposterously • stored • trailer* *keep track of • success story • on campus*	Statements in Reported Speech	Quoting Speech

SELF-TESTS

SELF-TEST 1: UNITS 1–8	PAGES **65–68**
SELF-TEST 2: UNITS 9–16	PAGES **134–137**

APPENDICES

INTERNET ACTIVITIES	PAGES **138–145**
MAP OF THE WORLD	PAGES **146–147**

INTRODUCTION

What a World: Amazing Stories from Around the Globe—the series

This series now has two strands: a listening strand and a reading strand. Both strands explore linked topics from around the world and across history. They can be used separately or together for maximum exploration of content and development of essential listening and reading skills.

	Listening Strand	**Reading Strand**
Level 1 (Beginning)	*What a World Listening 1*	*What a World Reading 1, 2e*
Level 2 (High-Beginning)	*What a World Listening 2*	*What a Word Reading 2, 2e*
Level 3 (Intermediate)	*What a World Listening 3*	*What a Word Reading 3, 2e*

What a World Listening 3—an intermediate listening and speaking skills book

It is the third in a three-book series of listening and speaking skills for English language learners. The sixteen units in this book correspond thematically with the units in *What a World Reading 3, 2e.* Each topic is about a different person, society, animal, place, custom, or organization. The topics span history and the globe, from famous castles around the world, to famous designers, to Oceania.

Unit Structure and Approach

BEFORE YOU LISTEN opens with a picture of the person, society, animal, place, custom, or organization featured in the unit. Prelistening questions follow. Their purpose is to motivate students to listen, encourage predictions about the content of the listening, and involve the students' own experiences when possible. Vocabulary can be presented as the need arises.

LONG TALK can be any one of a variety of scenarios, including a class lecture, a long conversation between two people, or a tour guide speaking to a group. The talk is about 350–400 words long. After an initial listening for general content, the teacher, at this point, may wish to explain the words in the vocabulary section. The students should then do a second, closer listening, perhaps in chunks. Further listening can be done depending on the students' requirements.

VOCABULARY exercises focus on the important topic-related words in the long talk. Both *Meaning* and *Words That Go Together* are definition exercises that encourage students to work out the meanings of words from the context. *Meaning* focuses on single words; *Words That Go Together* focuses on collocations or groups of words that are easier to learn together the way they are used in the language. The third exercise, *Use*, reinforces the vocabulary further by making students use the words or collocations in a meaningful, yet possibly different, context. This section can be done during or after the listening to the long talk, or both.

COMPREHENSION exercises appear in each unit and consist of *Understanding the Listening, Remembering Details,* and *Inference.* These confirm the content of the talk either in general, in detail, or by inference. These exercises for developing listening skills can be done individually, in pairs, in small groups, or as a class. It is preferable to do these exercises in conjunction with the long talk, since they are not meant to test memory.

TAKING NOTES is a fun feature where students listen to a short description of a place, person, or thing related to the unit. It is not necessary for students to understand every word, but they are encouraged to take notes. From their notes, they decide which of the two options they are given fits the description.

SHORT CONVERSATIONS consists of three new conversations related to the topic of the unit. The exercises focus on content as well as the speaker's tone and attitude, what the speaker is doing, the speaker's job, and where the conversation is taking place.

DISCUSSION questions encourage students to bring their own ideas and imagination to the related topics in each long talk. They can also provide insights into cultural similarities and differences.

CRITICAL THINKING questions give students the opportunity to develop thinking skills (comparing and contrasting cultural customs, recognizing personal attitudes and values, etc.).

LANGUAGE FOCUS draws on a grammatical structure from the listening and offers exercises to help students develop accuracy in speaking and writing. The exercises build from controlled to more open-ended.

PRONUNCIATION exercises focus on a recurring pronunciation feature in the unit. These exercises help students to hear and practice word endings, reductions, stress, and intonation.

CONVERSATION exercises start with a set conversation for students to listen to and repeat. Then students progress to a freer conversation that they create using new expressions from the set conversations.

Additional Activities

INTERNET ACTIVITIES (in the Appendices) give students the opportunity to develop their Internet research skills. Each activity can be done in a classroom setting or, if the students have Internet access, as homework leading to a presentation or discussion in class. There is an Internet activity for each unit and it is always related to the theme of the unit. It helps students evaluate websites for their reliability and gets them to process and put together the information in an organized way.

SELF-TESTS after Unit 8 and Unit 16 review general listening comprehension, vocabulary, and the grammar from the language focus in a multiple-choice format.

✳ ✳ ✳ ✳ ✳

The **Answer Key** for *What a World Listening 3* is available at the following website: http://www.pearsonlongman.com/whataworld.

WHAT ARE SOME FAMOUS CASTLES AROUND THE WORLD?

before you listen

Answer these questions.

1. What kind of image comes to mind when you hear the word "castle"?

2. Have you ever visited a castle? If so, which one? If not, what castle would you like to visit?

3. What would you expect a castle in California to look like?

VOCABULARY

MEANING

 Listen to the talk. Then write the correct words in the blanks.

acquired	design	excursion	impressive
besides	exasperating	hired	publisher

1. Architects _____ buildings by making detailed plans of a building's form and structure.

2. I _____ a painting of Windsor Castle from a friend who was moving and gave it to me.

3. My cousin did the most annoying things on our trip. He was _____.

4. The _____ of *Historic Places* magazine also produces history books.

5. I'm taking a short trip, or _____, to visit the most famous castles in Germany.

6. The amount of work they put into that building is _____; it's certainly worth going to see.

7. They _____ gardeners to plant flowers around the castle grounds.

8. _____ the flower beds, they also added a nice vegetable garden.

WORDS THAT GO TOGETHER

Write the correct words in the blanks.

guest list	historic sites	made his fortune

1. He _____—millions of dollars, in fact—by working hard.

2. These _____ are places where important things happened in the past.

3. My _____ includes the name and e-mail address of everyone coming to my party.

USE

Work with a partner to answer the questions. Use complete sentences.

1. What is an *impressive* building in your country?

2. How would you like to *make your fortune*?

3. What is an *excursion* that you sometimes take?

4. Who would you *hire* to help you with a project?

5. If you could put anyone on your dinner *guest list*, who would it be?

6. What kind of behavior do you find *exasperating*?

7. What is the best thing that you *acquired* this year?

8. What is something you *designed*? Describe it.

COMPREHENSION: LONG TALK

UNDERSTANDING THE LISTENING

Listen to the talk. Then circle the letter of the correct answer.

1. How did William Randolph Hearst become wealthy?
   a. He wrote books.
   b. He owned a company that published newspapers.
   c. He designed castles and other large buildings.

2. Why did it take twenty-eight years to build Hearst Castle?
   a. All the materials came from Europe.
   b. The architect had trouble creating the plans.
   c. Hearst had difficulty deciding what he wanted.

3. Why was Marie impressed by Hearst Castle?
   a. Because it had the world's largest private zoo.
   b. Because of its size and beauty.
   c. Because of the famous people who lived there.

REMEMBERING DETAILS

Listen to the talk again. Circle T if the sentence is true. Circle F if the sentence is false.

1. Hearst Castle is located in San Francisco.	T	F
2. Julia Morgan started working on the castle in 1919.	T	F
3. Hearst Castle is made up of four buildings that are each 60,000 square feet.	T	F
4. Hearst collected many antiques during his trips to Europe.	T	F
5. The castle has swimming pools, tennis courts, and a movie studio.	T	F
6. Many famous movie stars and society people lived at Hearst Castle.	T	F

INFERENCE

Circle the letter of the correct answer.

1. From the passage, what can we infer about Julia Morgan?
   a. She was a patient and talented architect.
   b. She didn't like working with Hearst.
   c. She didn't have enough experience to design such an extravagant place.

2. What can we conclude about Hearst Castle?
   a. It was too large for most guests to enjoy.
   b. It combined Hearst's European and American tastes.
   c. It's a strange place that is large but not very beautiful.

TAKING NOTES: Castles

 Listen and write notes about the description. Which castle does it describe?

Neuschwanstein Castle

Windsor Castle

COMPREHENSION: SHORT CONVERSATIONS

Listen to the conversations. Then circle the letter of the correct answer.

CONVERSATION 1

1. How does the man feel about his idea?
   a. enthusiastic   b. irritated   c. unsure

2. What does the woman want the man to do?
   a. sell his invention in   b. run for the train   c. hurry his packing
      a travel store

CONVERSATION 2

3. Where are the man and woman?

    a. at a travel agency   **b.** at a hotel   **c.** in their new apartment

4. What is the man's attitude?

    a. dissatisfied   **b.** impressed   **c.** pleased

CONVERSATION 3

5. Who is the man talking to?

    a. his tour guide   **b.** the hotel manager   **c.** his travel partner

6. How is the man feeling?

    a. worried   **b.** aggravated   **c.** amazed

DISCUSSION

Discuss the answers to these questions with your classmates.

1. What is the most impressive building you have ever visited? What did you like about it?
2. What building would you most like to see? Where is it located? Why would you like to see it?
3. Do you like to visit historic sites? Why or why not? What historic sites have you visited? Which ones would you like to see? Why?

CRITICAL THINKING

Work with a partner. Ask each other the following questions. Discuss your answers.

1. If you could design a castle for yourself, what would it be like? Explain your choices.
2. Wealthy people often build extravagant homes, or mansions, for themselves. What kinds of things do we find in such homes today? Would you like to live in a mansion? Why or why not? If you had a choice of building yourself a mansion or building 100 homes for other people, which would you choose and why?

 **L**ANGUAGE **F**OCUS

TAG QUESTIONS

Tag questions are short questions that are "tagged" on, or added, at the end of a sentence. We form them with the auxiliary verb from the first part of the sentence. The subject of the tag question is always a pronoun. When we write, we put a comma before a tag question. When the verb in the first part of the sentence is positive, we use a negative tag question. When the verb in the first part is negative, we use a positive tag question.

Positive Verb, Negative Tag		Negative Verb, Positive Tag	
Main Sentence	**Tag**	**Main Sentence**	**Tag**
It**'s** a museum,	**isn't it?**	It **isn't** a museum,	**is it?**
It **looks** breathtaking,	**doesn't it?**	It **doesn't look** breathtaking,	**does it?**
He **lived** there,	**didn't he?**	He **didn't live** there,	**did he?**
We **will visit** it again,	**won't we?**	We **won't visit** it again,	**will we?**
They **were** very helpful,	**weren't they?**	They **weren't** very helpful,	**were they?**

We use tag questions

- to check something we said in the first part of a sentence

   He was one of the richest men in the world, ***wasn't he?*** (The speaker is not sure and uses a tag to check.)

- to ask for agreement

   It's getting late, ***isn't it?*** (The speaker expects the answer yes.)
   You aren't tired, ***are you?*** (The speaker expects the answer no.)

A. *Complete the sentences. Write tag questions.*

EXAMPLE: You don't live there, *do you*?

   1. It took a long time to build, _____?

   2. He didn't know what he wanted, _____?

   3. She can't join the tour now, _____?

   4. He was a difficult man, _____?

   5. We will come again, _____?

   6. You won't be able to make it, _____?

B. *Work with a partner. Take turns asking and answering questions about Hearst Castle and other castles you know about. Use tag questions.*

EXAMPLE:

A: You want to visit Hearst Castle, don't you?

B: Yes, I do!

PRONUNCIATION

INTONATION FOR TAG QUESTIONS

When we are sure of the answer, the intonation falls in the tag question. When we're not sure of the answer, the intonation rises in the tag question.

A. *Listen to the sentences. Notice how the intonation falls or rises in the tag question. Listen again and repeat.*

1. It's in California, isn't it?

   He had a daughter, didn't he?

   She was a known architect, wasn't she?

2. It's in California, isn't it?

   He had a daughter, didn't he?

   She was a known architect, wasn't she?

B. *Listen to the questions. Circle **S** if the speaker is sure. Circle **US** if the speaker is unsure.*

1. S US
2. S US
3. S US
4. S US
5. S US
6. S US

CONVERSATION

A. *Listen to the conversation. Then listen again and repeat.*

Alma: Guess what? I'm taking an excursion to Italy next month.

Bart: That <u>sounds like fun</u>. You went there before, didn't you?

Alma: Yes, but Italy is <u>chock full of</u> historic sites, and I am a history major.

Bart: Right. I'm sure there's always more to see. Have you spent time in Venice?

Alma: Yes. I think it's <u>out of this world</u>. Hey, do you want to go with me?

Bart: I'd love to, but I need to study. I have exams coming up.

Alma: I see. Well, if you <u>change your mind</u>, let me know.

Do you know these expressions? What do you think they mean?

> sounds like fun   chock full of   out of this world   change your mind

B. *Work with a partner. Practice a part of the conversation. Replace the underlined words with the words below.*

Alma: Guess what? I'm taking an excursion to Italy next month.

Bart: That <u>sounds like fun</u>. You went there before, didn't you?

> is awesome   doesn't surprise me

C. Your Turn. *Write a new conversation. Use some of the words below and your own ideas. Practice the conversation with a partner.*

> change your mind   chock full of   out of this world   sounds like fun

Go to page 138 for the Internet Activity.

DID YOU KNOW?	• **Neuschwanstein Castle in Germany was the inspiration for Disneyland's Sleeping Beauty Castle.** • **Prague Castle in the Czech Republic is the world's largest castle and is now the site of the Summer Shakespeare Festival.** • **Himeji Castle, the most visited castle in Japan, is in the James Bond film *You Only Live Twice*, among other films.**

WHAT DO YOU KNOW ABOUT ANCIENT CIVILIZATIONS OF THE AMERICAS?

before you listen

Answer these questions.

1. What is a mysterious place in your country?
2. What are some ruins in your country?
3. What famous ruins would you like to see?

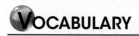

MEANING

Listen to the talk. Then write the correct words in the blanks.

anticipated	captured	conquering	revealing
astonishing	complex	massive	ruins

1. When the Spaniards were _____ the Mayans, they destroyed many of their cities.

2. Once they _____ a Mayan city, the Spaniards destroyed it and built one of their own.

3. One Mayan pyramid is _____. It is 12 stories tall and has 120 steps.

4. The _____ of houses was designed to allow people to have private space as well as be close to others.

5. The Mayan pyramids were _____ to us because they were so unusual and large.

6. I expected the weather in Peru to be very hot, but it turned out to be different than I _____.

7. The _____ of Templo Mayor are the physical remains of an Aztec temple in Mexico City.

8. The sun rose, _____ the beautiful buildings of the ancient city.

WORDS THAT GO TOGETHER

Write the correct words in the blanks.

above sea level	set off	settled in

1. After loading our backpacks, we _____ on the hike with everything we needed for the day.

2. The museum was built high on a hill, several thousand feet _____.

3. After the visitors _____ and stopped moving around, we started the lecture.

USE

Work with a partner to answer the questions. Use complete sentences.

1. What is the most *massive* structure you have ever seen?

2. What is the most *astonishing* historical fact you know?

3. Who do you usually *reveal* your secrets to?

4. What are the most famous *ruins* in your country?

5. What is something that did not turn out as you *anticipated*?

6. What *complex* of buildings do you often go to?

7. What would you need when *setting off* for a trip to Machu Picchu?

8. What bad habit of yours would you like to *conquer*?

COMPREHENSION: LONG TALK

UNDERSTANDING THE LISTENING

Listen to the talk. Then circle the letter of the correct answer.

1. Why did Hiram Bingham follow the man into the forest?
   a. He was looking for the ruins of Machu Picchu.
   b. He hoped to find the Incas' last capital.
   c. He saw some stone structures on the mountain.

2. What is mysterious about Machu Picchu?
   a. It was built above the misty forest.
   b. No one knows what materials were used to build it.
   c. No one knows why its inhabitants disappeared.

3. Why aren't most of the Inca cities still here today?
   a. The Spanish destroyed them.
   b. The Incas hid them.
   c. The Incas didn't build them to be very strong.

REMEMBERING DETAILS

Listen to the talk again. Then circle the letter of the correct answer.

1. Where are the ruins of Machu Picchu?
   a. Mexico   b. Peru   c. Brazil

2. Where did the Incas build Machu Picchu?
   a. at the top of a mountain   b. far down into a thick forest   c. along a river

(continued)

3. What was Machu Picchu built of?

    a. brick and mortar   **b.** wood from the forest   **c.** large stones

4. What do people think Machu Picchu was used for?

    a. religious ceremonies   **b.** enemy attacks   **c.** family living

5. What did the Spanish want from the Incas?

    a. slaves   **b.** cities   **c.** gold and silver

6. Why wasn't Machu Picchu destroyed?

    a. It didn't have anything the Spanish wanted.

    b. It was hidden by the forest.

    c. It was built after the Spanish left.

INFERENCE

Write **F** *if the sentence is a fact stated in the talk. Write* **I** *if the sentence can be inferred from the talk.*

1. _____ Bingham was a professor from Yale.

2. _____ Bingham never expected to find Machu Picchu.

3. _____ Machu Picchu was built in a place that was difficult to reach.

4. _____ The Incas ruled a huge empire.

5. _____ The Incas were good builders.

6. _____ The Spanish wanted to destroy the Inca culture.

TAKING NOTES: Vegetables

Listen and write notes about the description. Which vegetable does it describe?

corn

potatoes

COMPREHENSION: SHORT CONVERSATIONS

 Listen to the conversations. Then circle the letter of the correct answer.

CONVERSATION 1

1. Where is the man?

   a. in a bookstore   **b.** at a library   **c.** in a computer store

2. How is the man feeling?

   a. frustrated   **b.** confused   **c.** afraid

CONVERSATION 2

3. What is the woman probably doing?

   a. hiking up a mountain   **b.** walking along the beach   **c.** getting a checkup from her doctor

4. What is the man's attitude toward the woman?

   a. annoyed   **b.** caring   **c.** indifferent

CONVERSATION 3

5. Why is the woman concerned about the buildings on Main Street?

   a. They are too old.   **b.** They have nice shops in them.   **c.** There are plans to take them down.

6. What is the man's opinion?

   a. He agrees with the woman.   **b.** He disagrees with the woman.   **c.** He doesn't care.

DISCUSSION

Discuss the answers to these questions with your classmates.

1. Do you think there are still some undiscovered ruins of past civilizations? Where do you think they are?
2. Why were the Spanish more powerful than the Incas? What are some other cultures that were destroyed or nearly destroyed by their invaders?
3. How do you think Hiram Bingham felt when he discovered Machu Picchu? What great discovery would you like to make? Why?

CRITICAL THINKING

Work with a partner. Ask each other the following questions. Discuss your answers.

1. The Spanish not only took the Inca treasures but also destroyed their cities. Why do you think they did that? Other conquerors in history were careful not to destroy the countries they occupied. Which was the better strategy? Why?

2. Why is it important to find and research historic sites? What do they tell us about the past? What can we learn that might help us in the present?

LANGUAGE FOCUS

PARTICIPLES AS ADJECTIVES

We can use the present and the past participles of verbs as adjectives.

Base Form	Present Participle	Past Participle	Base Form	Present Participle	Past Participle
amaze	amazing	amazed	excite	exciting	excited
amuse	amusing	amused	frighten	frightening	frightened
annoy	annoying	annoyed	interest	interesting	interested
bore	boring	bored	relax	relaxing	relaxed
disappoint	disappointing	disappointed	surprise	surprising	surprised

- We use the past participle as adjectives to describe someone's feelings.

  *He was **excited** when they told him about the place.*

- To show what caused the feeling, we can use a prepositional phrase. Most participles take the preposition *by*. Others take other prepositions. For example, *interested* takes *in*.

  *They were **fascinated by** astrology.*
  *They were **interested in** astrology.*

- We use the present participle as adjectives to describe the person or thing that produces the feeling.

  It was an astonishing sight.

A. *Circle the correct word.*

1. The long trip was (tiring / tired).

2. The sight of the temple was (amazed / amazing).

3. We were (surprised / surprising) to see a sundial in the temple.

4. Scientists are (puzzling / puzzled) by how they carried the stones up the mountain.

5. The Spanish were (interested / interesting) in the Inca gold.

6. Machu Picchu is a (fascinating / fascinated) place.

B. *Write sentences using each of the participles as adjectives. Write opinions.*

EXAMPLE: <u>Guided tours are boring.</u>

- boring
- excited
- interested
- relaxing

_____

_____

_____

_____

PRONUNCIATION

THE SOUND BEIGE / ʒ /

A. *Listen to these words. Can you hear the different sounds of / ʒ / (zh) and / ʃ / (sh)? Then listen again and repeat.*

astonish   beige   television   decision

B. *Listen to the words. Check the words with the / ʒ / sound. Then say the words aloud.*

1. _____ Spanish
2. _____ decision
3. _____ usual
4. _____ television

5. _____ treasure
6. _____ ocean
7. _____ nation
8. _____ anxious

CONVERSATION

A. *Listen to the conversation. Then listen again and repeat.*

Diana: I can't wait to see those ruins. My excitement is almost <u>too much to bear</u>.

Cecil: They're not <u>far away</u>. It's only a short bus ride from here.

Diana: I just love a place that's <u>full of mystery</u>. <u>You see</u>, my great-grandparents were from this area, but I never knew them.

Cecil: That's so interesting!

Diana: I know. I just hope the weather is good when we set off for the ruins.

Cecil: I think it will be. It's not as hot as I anticipated. We came at the right time of year.

Do you know these expressions? What do you think they mean?

too much to bear   far away   full of mystery   you see

B. *Work with a partner. Practice a part of the conversation. Replace the underlined words with the words below.*

Diana: I just love a place that's full of mystery. <u>You see</u>, my great grandparents were from this area, but I never knew them.

Cecil: That's so interesting!

I haven't mentioned that   What you don't know is that

C. **Your Turn.** *Write a new conversation. Use some of the words below and your own ideas. Practice the conversation with a partner.*

far away   full of mystery   too much to bear   you see

Go to page 138 for the Internet Activity.

DID YOU KNOW?

- The llama was an important animal for the Incas because it could survive at over 10,000 feet (3,000 meters). The Incas used it for transportation and food, and to make clothes and blankets.
- The Incas made knots in string to keep records of past events.
- Built on top of pyramids, Mayan temples were faced with images of rulers that people could see from miles away.

WHAT ARE SOME FAMOUS FESTIVALS AROUND THE WORLD?

before you listen

Answer these questions.

1. What are some festivals in your country?
2. Which is your favorite festival?
3. What holiday or festival do you know that celebrates nature?

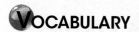

MEANING

🎧 *Listen to the talk. Then write the correct words in the blanks.*

entire	harvest	incense	reunions
fast	immortal	proceeded	tucked

1. The ancient Greeks believed that their gods were _____; that is, they lived forever.

2. He has worked his _____ life, since he was a child, for the good of others.

3. She _____ the box of chocolates inside her coat when it began to rain.

4. During the _____, farmers take their crops from the fields.

5. At family _____, people get together, have a picnic, and talk about old times.

6. After receiving her assignment, the reporter _____ to make travel plans, pack her clothes, and leave for the airport.

7. Because I had to _____ the entire day, I couldn't join my friends for lunch at the festival.

8. When we burned the _____, the smoke made a pleasant scent in the room.

WORDS THAT GO TOGETHER

Write the correct words in the blanks.

dates back to	in observance of	long for

1. After working hard, people _____ some time off.

2. This necklace _____ the 1920s, a time when my grandmother was young.

3. We had a party _____ the holiday, and everyone celebrated.

USE

Work with a partner to answer the questions. Use complete sentences.

1. What is a culture that burns *incense* as a custom?

2. What is something you have waited an *entire* year or more to get?

3. What things do people *tuck* and where do they *tuck* them?

4. What do you own that *dates back to* another time?

5. What is a reason why someone might *fast*?

6. Why do people celebrate *harvest* time?

7. What is something you do *in observance of* a holiday or special occasion?

8. Where do your family *reunions* usually take place?

 COMPREHENSION: LONG TALK

UNDERSTANDING THE LISTENING

Listen to the talk. Then circle the letter of the correct answer.

1. What is the main activity of the Moon Festival?

   a. getting together

   b. paying back debts

   c. making amends for wrongdoings

2. What do the Chinese do when they look at the moon on the fifteenth day?

   a. pray for a good harvest

   b. think good thoughts about others

   c. make plans for their future

3. Why did the Goddess of Western Heaven want Hou Yi to pray and fast?

   a. She wanted him to prepare to become immortal.

   b. She wanted him to get ready to shoot down the nine suns.

   c. She wanted to help him be a better husband.

REMEMBERING DETAILS

Listen to the talk again. Circle the letter of the correct answer.

1. When does the Moon Festival take place?

   a. in the winter   b. in the spring   c. in the autumn

2. What is another name for the Moon Festival?

   a. Harvest Festival   b. Lovers Festival   c. Mid-Autumn Festival

(continued)

3. What is a custom that is observed during the Moon Festival?

    a. lighting lanterns   **b.** eating special noodles   **c.** praying and fasting

4. What was happening to the earth during the time of the legend?

    a. It was extremely cold.   **b.** It was becoming hot.   **c.** It was always dark.

5. What did Hou Yi do with the special pill that the goddess gave him?

    a. He took it right away.   **b.** He hid it.   **c.** He lost it.

6. According to legend, what happens every year on the fifteenth day of the eighth month of the lunar calendar?

    a. The goddess punishes   **b.** Hou Yi shoots down   **c.** Hou Yi visits his wife.
        Hou Yi's wife.   nine suns.

INFERENCE

*Write **F** if the sentence is a fact stated in the talk. Write **I** if the sentence can be inferred from the talk.*

1. _____ The Moon Festival is an important Chinese holiday.

2. _____ The Moon Festival is also a celebration of the harvest.

3. _____ Families get together when the full moon rises.

4. _____ Not everyone celebrates the Moon Festival in the same way.

5. _____ Hou Yi was courageous and obedient.

6. _____ Hou Yi forgave his wife for what she did.

TAKING NOTES: Festivals

Listen and write notes about the description. Which festival does it describe?

Diwali Festival

Dragon Boat Festival

COMPREHENSION: SHORT CONVERSATIONS

Listen to the conversations. Then circle the letter of the correct answer.

CONVERSATION 1

1. Why does the woman want to go to Norway?

   a. to see her family
   b. to see her friend's family
   c. to attend an event

2. What will the man probably do?

   a. go to Norway
   b. stay where it's warm
   c. visit his family

CONVERSATION 2

3. What does the man have to decide?

   a. whether to cancel his plans
   b. whether to go with another plan
   c. a and b

4. What is the woman's attitude?

   a. apologetic
   b. upset
   c. rude

CONVERSATION 3

5. What does the woman want the man to do?

   a. stop baking
   b. give her a piece of cake
   c. take her to the evening festivities

6. What is the man's attitude toward the woman?

   a. considerate
   b. teasing
   c. angry

DISCUSSION

Discuss the answers to these questions with your classmates.

1. Would you like to be immortal? Why or why not? What are the advantages of immortality? What are the disadvantages?

2. Why is it important for families to get together? Do you enjoy family reunions? Why or why not?

3. What are some of your favorite customs during holidays? Why do you enjoy them? What customs in other cultures would you like to experience?

CRITICAL THINKING

Work with a partner. Ask each other the following questions. Discuss your answers.

1. Every culture has its own holidays and festivals. Why are these occasions important to society? What purposes do they serve? What would life be like without them?

2. What is romance? Are love and romance the same thing? Did Hou Yi love his wife? How do we know? Do love and forgiveness go together? Are some acts unforgivable?

LANGUAGE FOCUS

NON-ACTION VERBS

Non-action verbs describe a state. They are sometimes called stative verbs. We do not use these verbs in the progressive form.

Verbs of the senses and perception: feel, hear, see, smell, sound, taste

Verbs of mental states: believe, doubt, expect, forget, know, mean, realize, recognize, remember, suppose, think, understand

Verbs of possession: belong, have, own, possess

Verbs of feeling and emotion: adore, astonish, deserve, dislike, enjoy, envy, fear, hate, like, love, mind, please, prefer, surprise, want, wish

Verbs of measurement: contain, cost, equal, measure, weigh

Other verbs that express states: be, exist, owe, require, seem

Some verbs have an active and a stative meaning.

> **think:** *I think it is a good idea.* (think = believe)
> *I am thinking about it.* (thinking = considering)
> **have:** *He has a cell phone.* (have = possess)
> *They are having a good time.* (*Having* is used in the progressive form in certain expressions: *having a good / bad time; having breakfast / lunch / dinner; having a baby*)

A. *Complete the sentences with the simple present or present progressive form of the verbs.*

1. I _____ (think) about going to the carnival.

2. I _____ (love) to wear costumes.

3. I _____ (have) a beautiful costume from last year.

4. I _____ (want) to wear a mask.

5. I _____ (hear) it is a great carnival this year.

6. My friends _____ (have) a good time at the carnival right now.

B. *Work with a partner. Complete the sentences with the verbs. Make the sentences true for you. Take turns reading your sentences.*

believe   deserve   dislike   doubt   expect   know   love   prefer   think

1. I _____ I will be rich one day.
2. I _____ to get a good job.
3. I _____ I will have a large family.
4. I _____ living in this country.
5. I _____ to have a nice place to live.

PRONUNCIATION

SILENT LETTERS

A. *English words have many silent letters. These letters are not pronounced. Listen to the words. Underline the silent letter(s) in each word. Then listen again and repeat the words.*

1. listen
2. doubt
3. know
4. write
5. answer
6. autumn

B. *Listen to the words. Underline the silent letter(s) in each word. Then listen again and repeat the words.*

1. knee
2. scent
3. wrongdoing
4. debts
5. could
6. tomb

A. *Listen to the conversation. Then listen again and repeat.*

> **Ana:** Do you send cards to your <u>loved ones</u> on February 14?
>
> **Jen:** No, our custom is different in Korea. On February 14, only females give a gift of candy to males.
>
> **Ana:** <u>How interesting.</u> When do guys give something to girls they are <u>fond of</u>?
>
> **Jen:** March 14 is "White Day." Males give gifts to females on that day. And sometimes they confess their love.
>
> **Ana:** What happens to people who have no romantic partners? Do they stay <u>out of sight</u>?
>
> **Jen:** There's a day for them called "Black Day," on April 14. These people get together and eat Jajang noodles, which are black!

Do you know these expressions? What do you think they mean?

loved ones　　How interesting.　　fond of　　out of sight

B. *Work with a partner. Practice a part of the conversation. Replace the underlined words with the words below.*

> **Ana:** Do you send cards to your <u>loved ones</u> on February 14?
>
> **Jen:** No, our custom is different in Korea. On February 14, only females give a gift of candy to males.

friends　　family members

C. **Your Turn.** *Write a new conversation. Use some of the words below and your own ideas. Practice the conversation with a partner.*

fond of　　How interesting.　　loved ones　　out of sight

Go to page 139 for the Internet Activity.

DID YOU KNOW?	• At the Monkey Festival in Lopburi, Thailand, locals prepare a feast for the monkeys. • At La Tomatina, a late summer festival in the village of Buñol, Spain, locals and tourists throw tomatoes at each other in celebration of the summer tomato harvest. • In China, on the fifth day of the fifth month of the Chinese lunar year, people celebrate the Dragon Boat Festival with special food and boat races. The event began as a search for a drowned poet in 278 B.C.E.	

WHO ARE SOME FAMOUS LEGENDARY CHARACTERS?

before you listen

Answer these questions.

1. Who was, or is, a famous outlaw or rebel in your country?

2. Who were the heroes of the stories you heard as a child?

3. What do you know about Robin Hood?

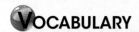

MEANING

Listen to the talk. Then write the correct words in the blanks.

abused	enforce	infamous	outlaw
corresponds	fugitive	manipulated	tyranny

1. After escaping from prison, the man lived as a(n) _____, changing his name and hiding from the sheriff.

2. The sheriff _____ the laws, changing them when his friends got into trouble.

3. The politician _____ her position by using the people's money improperly.

4. Jesse James was a famous _____ who went against the rules of society.

5. The professor demanded that her students come to class on time and was able to _____ the rule by failing those who didn't.

6. Everyone knew about the _____ criminal and his crimes.

7. The current decrease in support for the president _____ with rising unemployment.

8. After years of cruelty and injustice, the dictator's _____ ended with his death.

WORDS THAT GO TOGETHER

Write the correct words in the blanks.

based on	good-hearted	took over

1. The deputy _____ the jailhouse duties while the sheriff was ill.

2. The author's story is _____ her own experiences.

3. The _____ man offered to give shelter to the poor.

USE

Work with a partner to answer the questions. Use complete sentences.

1. What is one way that a leader can *abuse* his or her power?

2. Who do you know who is *good-hearted*?

3. Who is an *infamous* person from the past or present?

4. What is one way that principals *enforce* school rules?

5. What is one way that children *manipulate* their parents?

6. What book or movie is *based on* the life of a real person?

7. What's the best way to end the *tyranny* of a bad ruler?

8. Where can a *fugitive* go to escape the law?

COMPREHENSION: LONG TALK

UNDERSTANDING THE LISTENING

Listen to the talk. Then circle the letter of the correct answer.

1. Why did the poor dislike Prince John?
   a. He defeated King Richard and sent him away.
   b. He was a weak leader who didn't enforce the laws.
   c. He used his power to enrich himself and his friends.

2. Why was the Sheriff of Nottingham an enemy of Robin Hood?
   a. The sheriff taxed the people for his own use.
   b. The sheriff was a good-hearted man who hated thieves.
   c. The sheriff wanted to take King Richard's throne.

3. What was Robin Hood and other outlaws of this time trying to do?
   a. rebel against bad leaders
   b. become rich and powerful themselves
   c. defend the leaders against ordinary people

REMEMBERING DETAILS

*Listen to the talk again. Circle **T** if the sentence is true. Circle **F** if the sentence is false.*

1. King Richard spent many years fighting a war in the Far East.   T   F

2. Robin Hood wanted King Richard to save the people of England   T   F
   from Prince John.

3. Robin Hood lived in Sherwood Forest near Nottingham.   T   F

4. The Sheriff of Nottingham finally caught Robin Hood.   T   F

5. Many people think the character of Robin Hood is based on   T   F
   real people.

6. Robin Hood was the only outlaw who became a hero in his time.   T   F

INFERENCE

Circle the letter of the correct answer.

1. From this talk, what can we infer about Prince John?
   a. He was a selfish leader.
   b. He was much like his brother Richard.
   c. He had many friends and few enemies.

2. What can we conclude about Robin Hood?
   a. He defended the rights of ordinary people.
   b. He abused people for his own gain.
   c. He was a bad man who only pretended to be good.

TAKING NOTES: Legendary Characters

Listen and write notes about the description. Which legendary character does it describe?

King Arthur

William Tell

COMPREHENSION: SHORT CONVERSATIONS

Listen to the conversations. Then circle the letter of the correct answer.

CONVERSATION 1

1. How does the woman feel?
   a. alarmed   b. disappointed   c. understanding

2. Where is Carlos working now?
   a. at a bookstore   b. at a research company   c. at the university library

CONVERSATION 2

3. Where did the fugitive commit his crime?
   a. Argentina   b. France   c. South Africa

4. What is the man's attitude?

   a. amazement   **b.** pleasure   **c.** confusion

CONVERSATION 3

5. Why was the mayor arrested?

   a. She didn't pay her   **b.** She stole from the city.   **c.** She abused her power.
      personal taxes.

6. How is the man feeling?

   a. amazed   **b.** satisfied   **c.** saddened

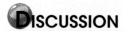DISCUSSION

Discuss the answers to these questions with your classmates.

1. What are the qualities of a hero? Who are some real-life heroes from the past or present? What were their heroic deeds? Why do people like to hear about heroes?

2. Fugitives are not always people fleeing from justice. Fugitives can also be people running from their enemies or from brutal treatment by an individual, group, or government. What are some examples of these types of fugitives, from the past or present? Explain what these people were running from and where they went.

3. Who are some famous outlaws from the American West or in your country? Were they kindhearted like Robin Hood? Were they fighting against tyranny? Why did they break the law? Were they heroes? Why or why not?

CRITICAL THINKING

Work with a partner. Ask each other the following questions. Discuss your answers.

1. Robin Hood stole from the rich and gave to the poor. Were his actions right or wrong? Why? Is there ever a good reason for doing something bad?

2. What are the qualities of a good leader? What are the faults of a bad leader? How can leadership corrupt even those who have the best intentions? Who are some good leaders in history? Who are some bad leaders?

USED TO AND WOULD + BASE VERB

Statements: *Used to*

Positive		Negative	
Subject	***used to* + Base Verb**	**Subject**	***didn't use to* + Base Verb**
I / You / He / She / It / We / They	**used to help** the poor.	I / You / He / She/ It / We / They	**didn't use to help** the poor.

Yes / No Questions: *Use to*

Question			Answer					
Did	**Subject**	***use to* + Base Verb**						
Did	I / you / he / she / it / we / they	**use to help** the poor?	Yes,	I / you / he / she / it / we / they	did.	No,	I / you / he / she / it / we / they	didn't.

Statements: *Would*

Subject	*would / would not*	
I / You / He / She / It / We / They	**would** **would not**	**help** the poor.

- We use *used to* when talking about a past habit that no longer occurs. We can also use the simple past (plus time) with no difference in meaning. We do not use *used to* when we give a specific time.

  INCORRECT: *William Tell used to be arrested in 1307.*
  CORRECT: *William Tell was arrested in 1307.*

- We can also use *would* instead of *used to* for a past habit. However, we cannot use *would* with stative verbs.

  INCORRECT: *King Richard would be in England for most of his reign.*
  CORRECT: *King Richard wasn't in England for most of his reign.*

- We often start a story in the past with *used to* and then continue with *would*.

A. *Underline the correct word.*

1. Robin Hood (was / would be) an English outlaw around 1200.

2. The people of Sherwood Forest (used to have / would have) the freedom to hunt when they pleased.

3. In 1225, there was a man who (was / used to be) a fugitive named Robert Hod.

4. Prince John (wasn't / wouldn't be) popular with the poor.

5. I (finished / used to finish) a book about Robin Hood last week.

6. Robin Hood (would / was) steal from the rich.

B. *Work with a partner. Take turns asking and answering questions about your lives now and your lives when you were children.*

EXAMPLE:
A: What programs did you use to watch on TV as a child?
B: I used to watch cartoons.

- TV shows / watch
- movies / like
- games / play
- places / like to go to
- food / like
- books / read

RONUNCIATION

THE *S* SOUND IN *USED TO* AND *USE / USED*

🎧 **A.** *Listen to the sentences. Notice the pronunciation of the letter s with the two usages of* use(d). *Then listen again and repeat the sentences.*

used to / didn't use to (*s* = / s /)
1. He used to live in England.
   People didn't use to travel far.

use / used (*s* = / z /)
2. I used my credit card.
   What will you use?

🎧 **B.** *Listen to the pronunciation of the letter s in the underlined words. Check the sound you hear.*

	/ s /	/ z /
1. They didn't <u>use</u> to have medicines.	____	____
2. I <u>used</u> to live in England.	____	____
3. I <u>used</u> a pencil.	____	____

(continued)

	/s/	/z/

4. He <u>used</u> to help the poor.   ____   ____

5. What dictionary do you <u>use</u>?   ____   ____

6. Does she <u>use</u> a microphone?   ____   ____

CONVERSATION

A. *Listen to the conversation. Then listen again and repeat.*

Ella: I heard your niece saw the new *Batman* movie. What did she think of it?

Franco: <u>As a matter of fact</u>, she loved it. It's very <u>popular with</u> teenagers.

Ella: Yes, I know. <u>Ordinary people</u> love to watch superheroes enforce the law.

Franco: Well, I don't think anyone is on the side of outlaws and fugitives, do you?

Ella: I hope not. But I'm still surprised Julie liked it. It's not her type of movie.

Franco: Maybe she's <u>tired of</u> comedies and romances. It's nice to see something different once in a while.

Do you know these expressions? What do you think they mean?

as a matter of fact   popular with   ordinary people   tired of

B. *Work with a partner. Practice a part of the conversation. Replace the underlined words with the words below.*

Ella: I heard your niece saw the new Batman movie. What did she think of it?

Franco: <u>As a matter of fact</u>, she loved it. It's very popular with teenagers.

I happen to know that   I'm pretty sure that

C. Your Turn. *Write a new conversation. Use some of the words below and your own ideas. Practice the conversation with a partner.*

as a matter of fact   ordinary people   popular with   tired of

Go to page 139 for the Internet Activity.

DID YOU KNOW?	• Stories about King Arthur exist going back before the eleventh century. Some people believe that King Arthur was a real person. Others believe his character is based on two or more real people.	

WHAT ARE SOME FAMOUS TEMPLES AROUND THE WORLD?

you listen

before

Answer these questions.

1. What are some important religious sites around the world?

2. Why do people like to visit ancient temples and other ruins?

3. What does it mean to be a World Heritage Site?

MEANING

🎧 *Listen to the talk. Then write the correct words in the blanks.*

academics	enlightenment	reliefs	restore
deserted	pilgrimage	replica	shrine

1. Some people try to find _____, or spiritual or religious understanding, through prayer and study.

2. I used wood polish to _____ the old chair to its original beauty.

3. Scholars, university teachers, and other _____ held a meeting to discuss global warming.

4. The model was an exact _____ of the Statue of Liberty.

5. The old _____ was the most beautiful place of worship that we saw on the entire trip.

6. Many people made the journey, or _____, to go see the holy place.

7. After the tourists left, the famous little town felt _____.

8. To create the _____, the artist carved the figures into a flat marble surface.

WORDS THAT GO TOGETHER

Write the correct words in the blanks.

bound by	place of worship	put together

1. In their _____, the people prayed and showed devotion to their god.

2. Because the countries were _____ their agreement, they had to follow the rules.

3. The preservation committee _____ a list of the area's most important historic buildings.

USE

Work with a partner to answer the questions. Use complete sentences.

1. What do touristic souvenir stores in your country sell *replicas* of?

2. What is a famous place that people make a *pilgrimage* to?

3. What places or areas in your country are *deserted*?

4. Where can people often see *reliefs*?

5. Where is there a famous *shrine*?

6. What kinds of things do builders do to *restore* an old building?

7. Where do *academics* spend much of their time?

8. Where is there a famous *place of worship*?

COMPREHENSION: LONG TALK

UNDERSTANDING THE LISTENING

Listen to the talk. Then circle the letter of the correct answer.

1. What is the mystery surrounding Borobudur?
   a. No one knows when it was built.
   b. No one knows how long it was hidden.
   c. No one knows why everyone left it.

2. What part did Sir Thomas Raffles play concerning Borobudur?
   a. He helped rediscover it.
   b. He restored it.
   c. He named it a World Heritage Site.

3. What do people think Borobudur is?
   a. a replica of the stars and planets
   b. an instruction on Buddhism
   c. an ancient city

REMEMBERING DETAILS

*Listen to the talk again. Circle **T** if the sentence is true. Circle **F** if the sentence is false.*

1. Borobudur was hidden for centuries under volcanic ash.	T	F
2. Sir Raffles was an archeologist in Java.	T	F
3. Borobudur is a textbook written by academics.	T	F
4. Borobudur has ten levels that represent the steps to enlightenment.	T	F

(continued)

5. Three levels represent the Buddhist universe.　　　　T　　F

6. The temple is no longer a place of worship.　　　　T　　F

INFERENCE

Circle the letter of the correct answer.

1. What can we infer about why Borobudur was built?
   a. It was a place where people lived and worked.
   b. It was a school for astronomers.
   c. It was a place for religious study.

2. From the conversation, what can we infer about the importance of Borobudur?
   a. It's appreciated mainly by Buddhists.
   b. It has lost its importance over the years.
   c. It's recognized by people around the world.

TAKING NOTES: Temples

 Listen and write notes about the description. Which temple does it describe?

Angkor Wat

Shwedagoni Pagoda

COMPREHENSION: SHORT CONVERSATIONS

Listen to the conversations. Then circle the letter of the correct answer.

CONVERSATION 1

1. How does the man feel?
   a. grateful　　　　b. proud　　　　c. surprised

2. Who is the man speaking to?
   a. an architect　　　　b. a student　　　　c. a teacher

CONVERSATION 2

3. What is the man's attitude?

   a. curious   **b.** upset   **c.** supportive

4. What does the woman have to do in order to finish her project?

   a. sand the table   **b.** repair the cracks   **c.** paint the table

CONVERSATION 3

5. What is the tourist worried about?

   a. the long walk   **b.** the heat   **c.** the climb

6. What is the tour guide's tone of voice?

   a. worried   **b.** encouraging   **c.** unsure

ISCUSSION

Discuss the answers to these questions with your classmates.

1. What is the function and purpose of archeology? Is the work of archeologists important? Why or why not?

2. What is an important ancient site in your country? Where is it? What does it look like? What purpose did it once serve?

3. Why is Borobudur so extraordinary? Would you want to visit Borobudur? Why or why not?

CRITICAL THINKING

Work with a partner. Ask each other the following questions. Discuss your answers.

1. How are ancient ruins restored and preserved? Why is it important for all nations to join together to preserve ancient sites? What is the purpose of listing an area as a World Heritage Site? What are some other World Heritage Sites?

2. Why do people make pilgrimages? What is the purpose of a pilgrimage? Why is it important to some people to make one or more pilgrimages in their lives? What important thing do you want to do or see in your life?

LANGUAGE FOCUS

PASSIVE VOICE

Verb Form	Active Voice	Passive Voice
simple present	The monument amazes visitors.	Visitors **are amazed** by the monument.
simple past	The monument amazed visitors.	Visitors **were amazed** by the monument.
present perfect	The monument has amazed visitors.	Visitors **have been amazed** by the monument.
future	The monument will amaze visitors.	Visitors **will be amazed** by the monument.

- We use the passive voice when we do not know who does the action, or it is not necessary to say who does it. We use the passive voice plus a *by* phrase when we want to focus on the subject but also include the person who did the action.

  *The Taj Mahal **was built** (by people) as a tomb.* (It is not important or necessary to say *by people*.)

A. *Complete the sentences with the correct form of the verbs. Use the active and passive voice when necessary. Some verbs are intransitive and cannot be passive.*

The Great Pyramid _____ (be) the largest of the monuments in the desert at
                         1.

Giza in Egypt. It _____ (built) over a period of twenty years. It
                  2.

_____ (finished) around 2560 B.C.E. Originally, the building _____
   3.   **4.**

(be) taller than a 40-story building. It _____ (make) of over 2 million stone
                                5.

blocks; each block _____ (weigh) about 2.5 tons. Today, visitors
                  6.

_____ (strike) with awe when they _____ (see) it. The building of
   7.   **8.**

the pyramid _____ (not carry out) by slaves. It _____ (do) by
             9.   **10.**

hundreds of thousands of ordinary people. They _____ (be expected) by their
                                   11.

ruler to offer their services when the Nile River flooded each year. Many skilled people such as

architects and engineers _____ (hire) to build a pyramid as well. In the past,
                          12.

people _____ (amaze) by it, and in the future, they _____ (be
       13.   **14.**

amazed) by it.

B. *Work with a partner. Write five sentences about famous monuments that you know. Use the passive voice.*

EXAMPLE:

The Eiffel Tower is named after Gustave Eiffel. When it was built, it was the tallest
building in the world.

1. _____
2. _____
3. _____
4. _____
5. _____

PRONUNCIATION

SENTENCE INTONATION AND STRESS

A. *Listen to the two questions. Notice the change in intonation and stress. Listen again and repeat the sentences.*

<u>Who</u> took this photo?

Who was this photo <u>taken by</u>?

B. *Listen to the sentences. Underline the stressed words.*

1. Who built this temple?
2. Who was this temple built by?
3. When will the tour finish?
4. When will the tour be finished by?
5. Where can I repair my camera?
6. Where can my camera be repaired?

CONVERSATION

A. *Listen to the conversation. Then listen again and repeat.*

Yousef: Did your travel agent help you with vacation plans yesterday?

Hasan: Yes, she was <u>more than happy to help</u>. I told her I wanted to go to Angkor Wat, but she said it's a big <u>tourist attraction</u> now.

(continued)

Yousef: <u>I didn't know that.</u> Vacation is about going someplace where there aren't many people.

Hasan: <u>You're exactly right.</u> But it looks like a quiet place is hard to find these days.

Do you know these expressions? What do you think they mean?

more than happy to help   tourist attraction   I didn't know that.   You're exactly right.

B. *Work with a partner. Practice a part of the conversation. Replace the underlined words with the words below.*

Yousef: <u>I didn't know that.</u> Vacation is about going someplace where there aren't many people.

Hasan: You're exactly right. But it looks like a quiet place is hard to find these days.

I had no idea.   I'm so surprised.

C. Your Turn. *Write a new conversation. Use some of the words below and your own ideas. Practice the conversation with a partner.*

I didn't know that.   more than happy to help   tourist attraction   You're exactly right.

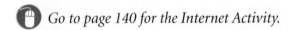 *Go to page 140 for the Internet Activity.*

DID YOU KNOW?

- The Buddhist temple of Horyuji at Nara in Japan is the oldest wooden building in the world, built around 600. It is built without using any screws, nails, or glue.
- One of the largest and oldest temples in the world is the Temple of Amun at Karnak, Egypt, built in 1539 B.C.E. It has been called a "stone forest" because of its 134 stone columns, which measure between 42 and 69 feet in height.
- The Baha'i House of Worship in New Delhi, India, is in the shape of a half-opened lotus and is called the Lotus Temple.

WHO ARE SOME FAMOUS FASHION DESIGNERS?

before you listen

Answer these questions.

1. Who is your favorite fashion designer?
2. What trendy clothes do you like to wear?
3. What cities come to mind when you think of fashion?

VOCABULARY

MEANING

Listen to the talk. Then write the correct words in the blanks.

bold	determined	garment	trendsetter
boutique	freelance	prestigious	will

1. She likes the new _____ because of its small size and fashionable clothes.

2. I don't usually like _____ colors, but that orange and red dress is beautiful.

3. My friend is a _____—everything she wears suddenly becomes popular.

4. He wanted to do what was right but was forced to act against his own _____.

5. He wanted to be a _____ photographer because he liked the idea of working for himself.

6. Working as a designer's assistant is an important but not very _____ job.

7. My aunt can sew any _____, from a simple dress to a three-piece suit, in less than a day.

8. She was _____ to become a fashion editor, so she put her mind to achieving her goal.

WORDS THAT GO TOGETHER

Write the correct words in the blanks.

end up	flea market	paved the way

1. That outdoor _____ sells an amazing amount of different things.

2. As a designer in the 1800s, she _____ for us, making it possible for women to do this job.

3. Where do you want to _____ after you finish your travels?

USE

Work with a partner to answer the questions. Use complete sentences.

1. Why do people like to go to *flea markets*?
2. Which *garment* in your closet is your favorite?
3. Why is it *prestigious* to go to the University of Oxford?
4. Where is your favorite *boutique* located?
5. Who was a *trendsetter* in early rock music?
6. What is one thing that you are *determined* to do in your life?
7. Why do some people like to do *freelance* work?
8. Who is someone who *paved the way* for others?

COMPREHENSION: LONG TALK

UNDERSTANDING THE LISTENING

Listen to the talk. Then circle the letter of the correct answer.

1. Why was it so unusual for Takada Kenzo to attend the fashion college in Tokyo?
   a. Males didn't study fashion in Japan.
   b. No one had ever heard of him before.
   c. He was the first student who had been to Paris.

2. How did Kenzo get his career started in Paris?
   a. He joined a group of other Japanese designers.
   b. He took his designs around to different fashion houses.
   c. He sold his designs at a flea market.

3. What did Kenzo do that other Paris designers were not doing?
   a. He combined different designs and fabrics.
   b. He made Japanese kimonos.
   c. He used dark colors and simple lines.

REMEMBERING DETAILS

Listen to the talk again. Circle the letter of the correct answer.

1. Where in Japan was Kenzo born?

   a. Himeji   **b.** Tokyo   **c.** Kobe

2. What did Kenzo study at the University of Kobe?

   a. fashion   **b.** literature   **c.** history

3. What did Kenzo do when he arrived in Tokyo?

   a. worked and took night classes   **b.** studied literature at a university   **c.** taught at a fashion college

4. How long did Kenzo plan to stay in Paris?

   a. six months   **b.** four years   **c.** forever

5. In Paris, what was difficult for Kenzo?

   a. getting a job   **b.** making designs   **c.** working for himself

6. What did Kenzo make his first garments from?

   a. designer fabrics   **b.** Japanese fabrics   **c.** bits and pieces of fabrics

INFERENCE

*Write **F** if the sentence is a fact stated in the talk. Write **I** if the sentence can be inferred from the talk.*

1. _____ Kenzo was the first Japanese designer to receive recognition in Paris.
2. _____ Kenzo showed an interest in fashion when he was very young.
3. _____ Kenzo showed courage when he left the University of Kobe.
4. _____ Kenzo's designs weren't initially celebrated by the fashion houses in Paris.
5. _____ Kenzo didn't have enough money to buy expensive fabrics.
6. _____ Kenzo's success was the result of years of hard work.

TAKING NOTES: Designers

🎧 *Listen and write notes about the description. Which designer does it describe?*

Tommy Hilfiger

Ralph Lauren

COMPREHENSION: SHORT CONVERSATIONS

🎧 *Listen to the conversations. Then circle the letter of the correct answer.*

CONVERSATION 1

1. What does the boutique owner want the designer to do?
   - **a.** earn some money
   - **b.** buy things from her boutique
   - **c.** sell things at a flea market

2. How does the designer feel?
   - **a.** appreciative
   - **b.** embarrassed
   - **c.** bored

CONVERSATION 2

3. Why is Mr. Sims upset?
   - **a.** His agent gave him the wrong information.
   - **b.** His agent isn't being helpful.
   - **c.** He went to Hawaii instead of Canada.

4. What is Mr. Sims's attitude?
   - **a.** apologetic
   - **b.** aggravated
   - **c.** fearful

CONVERSATION 3

5. What is the woman's tone?
   - **a.** sarcastic
   - **b.** annoyed
   - **c.** sad

6. What is the man telling the woman?
   - **a.** It's her fault that she failed her test.
   - **b.** It's his fault that they failed their tests.
   - **c.** No one is to blame for failing their tests.

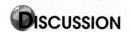

DISCUSSION

Discuss the answers to these questions with your classmates.

1. What are the latest trends in fashion today? Which ones do you like? Which ones don't you like? Why?

2. Is it important for you to wear fashionable clothing? Why or why not? What are the positive aspects of keeping up with the latest fashion trends? What are the negative aspects?

3. What fashion trends do you foresee for the future? How will they be different from today's fashions?

CRITICAL THINKING

Work with a partner. Take turns asking each other the following questions. Discuss your answers.

1. Who are some people who have paved the way for others? Why do people admire those who make a path for others to follow? What characteristics do such people have in common? Are you a trendsetter or do you prefer to follow the trends? Why?

2. Kenzo's success didn't come quickly or easily. Do you think this is true of most successful people? Why? What does it mean to "pay your dues"? Would you prefer to have "instant" fame or success, or would you rather work for it? Why?

LANGUAGE FOCUS

PAST PERFECT

Action 1			Action 2
I / You / He / She / It / We / They	'd (had) heard hadn't heard	of him	until he appeared on TV last week.

- We use the past perfect tense to express an action in the past that happened before another action in the past. We use the past perfect for the first action in time and the simple past for the second action.

      Action 2   **Action 1**

  *By the time he **returned** to his country, he **had become** world famous.*

- The past perfect can come before the simple past verb. The verb tense shows which action came first.

      Action 1   **Action 2**

  *He **had become** famous by the time he **returned**.*

A. *Complete the sentences with the simple past or past perfect form of the verbs.*

Coco Chanel _____ (start) with a small hat shop in Paris and then
1.
_____ (begin) to make clothes. By 1920, her fashion house _____
2.   3.
(expand), and she _____ (launch) a fashion trend. Two years later, she
4.
_____ (introduce) a perfume called Chanel No. 5, which soon
5.
_____ (become) popular. By the time she died in 1971, she _____
6.   7.
(create) not only suits and dresses, but also perfumes and textiles; she _____
8.
(revolutionize) women's fashions.

B. *Work with a partner. Choose a particular age in your past. Then say four experiences you had had by that age. Tell them to your partner. Compare your experiences.*

EXAMPLE: By the time I was fourteen, I had traveled to three cities in my country.

PRONUNCIATION

LINKING *'D* IN THE PAST PERFECT TENSE

A. *Listen to the sentences. Can you hear the contraction of* had? *Then listen again and repeat.*

1. He wanted to be a designer.   2. She opened her boutique.

   He'd wanted to be a designer.   She'd opened her boutique.

B. *Listen to the sentences. Circle the letter of the one you hear.*

1. **a.** He decided to go to college.   **b.** He'd decided to go to college.
2. **a.** She changed women's clothes.   **b.** She'd changed women's clothes.
3. **a.** He created a new trend.   **b.** He'd created a new trend.
4. **a.** I never heard of him.   **b.** I'd never heard of him.
5. **a.** She paved the way for others.   **b.** She'd paved the way for others.
6. **a.** He designed ties.   **b.** He'd designed ties.

A. *Listen to the conversation. Then listen again and repeat.*

Iliana: I've decided to <u>take classes</u> in drama. I'm determined to be an actor.

Javier: What? Are you serious?

Iliana: Yes! You know, I showed an interest in acting <u>at an early age</u>. To this day, I haven't stopped thinking about it.

Javier: Well, <u>at least</u> you have a business degree to back you up.

Iliana: That doesn't show much faith in me! <u>Anyway</u>, I know I'll succeed.

Javier: Then I wish you all the best. I mean it. I hope you become a star.

Do you know these expressions? What do you think they mean?

take classes   at an early age   at least   anyway

B. *Work with a partner. Practice a part of the conversation. Replace the underlined words with the words below.*

Javier: Well, <u>at least</u> you have a business degree to back you up.

Iliana: That doesn't show much faith in me! Anyway, I know I'll succeed.

in any case,   you're lucky that

C. Your Turn. *Write a new conversation. Use some of the words below and your own ideas. Practice the conversation with a partner.*

anyway   at an early age   at least   take classes

Go to page 140 for the Internet Activity.

| DID YOU KNOW? | • It is believed that one of the first popular brand names to appear on the outside of an article of clothing was the Lacoste "crocodile" in 1933, created by the French tennis champion René Lacoste.
• The perfume Chanel No. 5 was created for Coco Chanel on the fifth day of the fifth month in 1921. It was said that the number five was Chanel's lucky number.
• American designer Tommy Hilfiger started his career by buying and selling blue jeans. |  |

HOW DO PEOPLE AROUND THE WORLD EAT?

you listen

Answer these questions.

1. In what countries do people eat with knives, forks, and spoons? Chopsticks? Their fingers?

2. Do you know the rules of etiquette in any countries other than your own? Why is it important to know another country's manners?

3. What problems might occur if you don't know the rules of etiquette in another country?

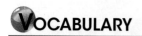

MEANING

Listen to the talk. Then write the correct words in the blanks.

belch	inappropriate	offend	slurp
etiquette	indicate	punctuality	utensils

1. In order to _____ his appreciation of the meal, the man sent the family a thank-you note.

2. Drinking club soda makes you _____, which some people believe calms an upset stomach.

3. My friend is always on time because she believes in _____.

4. Ned shocked everyone when he began to loudly _____, rather than sip, his tea.

5. Pablo's casual clothes were _____ for the formal occasion, so he looked out of place.

6. Good manners in one country are not always proper _____ in another.

7. It's easy to _____ and insult people in other countries when we don't know their culture.

8. Looking at the two knives, two forks, and spoon before her, the guest felt confused by the number of _____.

WORDS THAT GO TOGETHER

Write the correct words in the blanks.

a crash course	fit in	make a good impression

1. She wanted her employer to think highly of her, so she worked hard in order to

   _____.

2. In order to _____ and be accepted, Carl learned all about the country he was visiting.

3. I leave for Albania in a very short time, so I need to take _____ in Albanian.

USE

Work with a partner to answer the questions. Use complete sentences.

1. When might someone want to *make a good impression*?
2. Why is it easy to *offend* someone from another culture?
3. When might you need to take *a crash course* in something?
4. What behavior is considered *inappropriate* for dinner guests in your country?
5. What is an example of good dining *etiquette* in your country?
6. Which *utensils* are used for eating in your culture?
7. What is something a visitor could do to *fit in* while visiting your country?
8. When is *punctuality* important in your country?

COMPREHENSION: LONG TALK

UNDERSTANDING THE LISTENING

Listen to the talk. Then circle the letter of the correct answer.

1. Why is Faaria upset when she arrives at her host's house?
   a. She's afraid she'll lose her job.
   b. She's late for dinner.
   c. She's there at an inappropriate time.

2. What is Faaria's reaction to the host's advice about international etiquette?
   a. She's confident.
   b. She's angry.
   c. She's overwhelmed.

3. What assurance does the host give to Faaria?
   a. The rules will become very familiar.
   b. She won't lose her job.
   c. She won't go to China.

REMEMBERING DETAILS

*Listen to the talk again. Circle **T** if the sentence is true. Circle **F** if the sentence is false.*

1. Faaria's host is an American living in the Middle East. T F

2. In the Middle East, it is best to leave some food on your plate. T F

(continued)

3. In Germany, you should try to eat all the food your host serves.　　T　　F

4. In Denmark, it's polite to arrive late for dinner.　　T　　F

5. The English use their utensils for almost all food.　　T　　F

6. In China, you should never belch at the table.　　T　　F

INFERENCE

Circle the letter of the correct answer.

1. From the passage, what can we infer about the host?
 a. She has sympathy for Faaria.
 b. She doesn't understand Faaria.
 c. She doesn't think etiquette is important.

2. What can we conclude about Faaria?
 a. She doesn't like her job.
 b. Her job is important to her.
 c. She will probably fail at her job.

TAKING NOTES: Utensils

🎧 *Listen and write notes about the description. Which utensil does it describe?*

fork　　　　　　　　spoon

COMPREHENSION: SHORT CONVERSATIONS

🎧 *Listen to the conversations. Then circle the letter of the correct answer.*

CONVERSATION 1

1. What is the restaurant manager's attitude?
 a. sympathetic　　　　**b.** matter-of-fact　　　　**c.** arrogant

2. What does the customer want the manager to do?

    a. help him find his wallet

    b. give him proper identification

    c. accept his check

CONVERSATION 2

3. Who is the woman talking to?

    a. her boss

    b. her coworker

    c. her teacher

4. What is the woman's tone of voice?

    a. teasing

    b. envious

    c. bitter

CONVERSATION 3

5. How does the woman feel?

    a. upset

    b. confused

    c. excited

6. Where is the couple?

    a. in a clothing store

    b. at the movies

    c. at a restaurant

DISCUSSION

Discuss the answers to these questions with your classmates.

1. What are some common rules of dining etiquette in your country? Does your family have any specific rules of dining etiquette? If so, what are they?
2. Where do you think rules of etiquette came from? What is their purpose? Why are they important?
3. What is hospitality? Is it important in your culture? How do people in your country show their hospitality? How would you describe a good host? A good guest?

CRITICAL THINKING

Work with a partner. Ask each other the following questions. Discuss your answers.

1. How might being well-mannered help a person to succeed in both personal and professional areas of life? If you don't understand the proper dining etiquette in your host's country, how can that be harmful to your relationship? Give examples.
2. Why is eating meals together an important opportunity to make friends and form bonds? How and when do you think this custom started? Do you eat meals with others regularly? Why or why not?

LANGUAGE FOCUS

SO THAT, IN ORDER TO

Clauses of purpose: *so that* . . .

We use clauses of purpose to answer the question *what for?* and *for what purpose?* *So that* is a common way to introduce the clause of purpose. When we speak, we can omit *that*.

> *I learned Spanish **so (that)** I could communicate with my new neighbor.*

In order to + **base verb**

We can also use *in order to* for purpose. It is a phrase of purpose, not a clause.

> *Nejma used utensils at dinner **in order to** fit in.*

A. *Join the two sentences with the words of purpose.*

EXAMPLE:

Learn how to say "please" and "thank you." Be polite. (in order to)

Learn how to say "please" and "thank you" in order to be polite.

1. They give you a bowl of water. You can wash your fingers after the meal. (so that)

   _____

2. When you are in England, eat all the food on your plate. Be polite to your host. (in order to)

   _____

3. Always say that the food was delicious. The person who cooked it feels good. (so that)

   _____

4. Don't forget to arrive on time. Give a good impression. (in order to)

   _____

5. Dress appropriately for the occasion. People with you do not feel embarrassed. (so that)

_____

6. Don't talk about controversial topics at the table. Show respect. (in order to)

_____

B. *Work with a partner. Take turns talking about what is important for you. Use* so that *or* in order to *for purpose.*

EXAMPLE: Wash your hands in order to stay healthy.

- stay healthy
- make friends
- keep friends
- be successful
- speak English well
- be polite

PRONUNCIATION

THE SOUNDS *SHERRY* / ʃ / AND *CHERRY* / tʃ /

A. *Listen to the following words. Notice the* ʃ *and* tʃ *sounds. Listen again and repeat the words.*

1. sherry / ʃ /   2. wash / ʃ /   3. chip / tʃ /

   cherry / tʃ /   watch / tʃ /   ship / ʃ /

B. *Listen to the words. Circle the one you hear.*

1. chop / shop   3. shin / chin   5. sheep / cheap

2. catch / cash   4. which / wish   6. shoes / choose

CONVERSATION

A. *Listen to the conversation. Then listen again and repeat.*

Lucy: My relatives from Guatemala are coming to visit in six months.

Marta: That's nice. Do you speak Spanish?

Lucy: <u>Not really.</u> I'm so embarrassed because everyone in my family speaks Spanish except me.

Marta: <u>Don't feel bad.</u> After all, you were born here in America. Do you want some help?

Lucy: Yes! Can you give me a crash course so that I won't offend anyone?

(continued)

Marta: Of course. In six months, you'll <u>know Spanish like the back of your hand</u>.

Lucy: <u>I hope so.</u>

Do you know these expressions? What do you think they mean?

Not really.   Don't feel bad.   know (something) like the back of your hand   I hope so.

B. *Work with a partner. Practice a part of the conversation. Replace the underlined words with the words below.*

Lucy: Yes! Can you give me a crash course so that I won't offend anyone?

Marta: Of course. In six months, you'll <u>know Spanish like the back of your hand</u>.

speak as well as they do   be talking like a native speaker

C. Your Turn. *Write a new conversation. Use some of the words below and your own ideas. Practice the conversation with a partner.*

Don't feel bad.   I hope so.   know (something) like the back of your hand   Not really.

Go to page 141 for the Internet Activity.

DID YOU KNOW?	• Buffalo wings, an American appetizer, have nothing to do with buffalo. They are spicy chicken wings that originated in Buffalo, New York. • *Guineo* is a green, banana-like fruit used in South American and Caribbean dishes including soup. • "Salsa" is Spanish for "sauce."

HOW DO PEOPLE CELEBRATE A WEDDING?

before

you listen

Answer these questions.

1. Where do wedding ceremonies usually take place in your culture?

2. What do the bride and groom wear? What do guests wear?

3. How long do the wedding celebrations last?

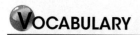

MEANING

 Listen to the talk. Then write the correct words in the blanks.

affairs	devotion	gown	reception
consider	fidelity	locals	union

1. As the bride and groom exchanged vows, we could all see the love and
   _____ in their eyes.

2. Asheville is a beautiful location for a wedding, but I wonder how the
   _____ feel about so many visitors in their town?

3. Some people _____ their wedding day to be the most important day of
   their lives.

4. Because we believe _____ is the key to a healthy marriage, we've
   resolved to be faithful partners.

5. Now that our two families have joined together, we have a strong _____
   among our members.

6. The party after the wedding was the best _____ I have ever attended.

7. I like to attend social events because I meet new people at these _____.

8. The full-length, blue dress made the perfect wedding _____.

WORDS THAT GO TOGETHER

Write the correct words in the blanks.

familiar with	give their blessings	run across

1. You may _____ something valuable if you go to enough flea markets.

2. When religious figures _____, they ask for divine help for someone.

3. I'm not _____ Native American wedding celebrations but would like
   to learn about them.

USE

Work with a partner to answer the questions. Use complete sentences.

1. What kinds of wedding traditions are you *familiar with*?

2. On what occasion do people promise *fidelity*?

3. Where is a good place to have a wedding *reception*?

4. What is an event that the *locals* in your town attend?

5. How does a mother show her *devotion* to her child?

6. What is the key to a happy *union*?

7. What fabric might a *gown* be made from?

8. What kinds of social *affairs* do you like to attend?

COMPREHENSION: LONG TALK

UNDERSTANDING THE LISTENING

Listen to the talk. Then circle the letter of the correct answer.

1. What do Chinese couples do to show their faithfulness?
   a. go to a park and wish each other good luck
   b. have a video made
   c. give each other a special handkerchief

2. How does a Sikh groom marry his bride?
   a. by handing her one end of a cloth
   b. by leading her around a holy book
   c. by placing a red turban on her head

3. What might a bride do during an Irish wedding?
   a. ask for gifts for the home
   b. throw flowers at the locals
   c. wear special colors

REMEMBERING DETAILS

Listen to the talk again. Circle the letter of the correct answer.

1. In China, what are ducks a symbol of?
   a. faithfulness   b. long life   c. prosperity

2. How long do wedding celebrations often last in India?
   a. a week   b. several weeks   c. a month

3. What color is the dress of a Sikh bride?
   a. cream-colored   b. red   c. white

(continued)

4. What do Sikh priests give to the bride and groom?

    a. a long cloth   **b.** advice   **c.** a holy book

5. How long does an American reception usually last?

    a. one day   **b.** a day and a night   **c.** several hours

6. What do an Irish bride's parents present her with?

    a. a blue gown   **b.** lavender flowers   **c.** pots and pans

INFERENCE

*Write **F** if the sentence is a fact stated in the talk. Write **I** if the sentence can be inferred from the talk.*

1. _____ Chinese couples combine modern and traditional customs at their weddings.
2. _____ In India, wedding celebrations are usually elaborate.
3. _____ For Sikhs, the family into which their child marries is very important.
4. _____ People stay longer at Latin American weddings than at American weddings.
5. _____ In Ireland, blue is a symbol of purity.
6. _____ In Ireland, the locals throw rice on the bride and groom.

TAKING NOTES: Brides

Listen and write notes about the description. Which bride does it describe?

Indian bride

Vietnamese bride

COMPREHENSION: SHORT CONVERSATIONS

Listen to the conversations. Then circle the letter of the correct answer.

CONVERSATION 1

1. What is the customer's problem?
   - **a.** She can't find a wedding gift.
   - **b.** The gift she wants is full price today.
   - **c.** She doesn't know what she wants to buy as a gift.

2. What is the salesperson like?
   - **a.** helpful
   - **b.** rude
   - **c.** anxious

CONVERSATION 2

3. How is the man feeling?
   - **a.** confused
   - **b.** depressed
   - **c.** relieved

4. What does the woman think the man should do?
   - **a.** go to the beach
   - **b.** travel to that area at another time
   - **c.** not visit that place ever again

CONVERSATION 3

5. Where are the man and woman?
   - **a.** in a hotel
   - **b.** on a beach
   - **c.** in a shop

6. What is the woman's attitude?
   - **a.** upset
   - **b.** undecided
   - **c.** impatient

DISCUSSION

Discuss the answers to these questions with your classmates.

1. What special colors does a bridal couple wear in your culture? What do the colors symbolize?
2. What is an interesting wedding ritual in your culture, and what is its meaning?
3. In your culture, what are some wedding customs that are considered good luck? What are some things that are thought to bring bad luck? Do you believe in these things? Why or why not?

Work with a partner. Ask each other the following questions. Discuss your answers.

1. What roles do the two families play in weddings in your culture? If you were thinking of getting married, how important would your spouse's family be to you? Could they influence your decision to get married? Why or why not? How do in-laws help a newly married couple? How do they make problems for them?

2. In your culture, does the groom ask his bride's father for permission to marry her? Do you approve or disapprove of this tradition? Why? What wedding customs in your culture do you think should continue? What customs do you think should be stopped? Why?

LANGUAGE FOCUS

MAY, MIGHT, COULD FOR POSSIBILITY (REVIEW); MAYBE OR MAY BE

May, might, and could: Present tense

Subject	Modal	Verb
I / You / He / She / It / We / They	may / may not might / might not could	send cards.

- We use *may, might,* and *could* to talk about possibility in the future.

  They **may / might / could** *get married in June.*
- We use *may not* and *might not* to say what possibly will not happen.

  The wedding **may not / might not** *take place.*
- Note that when talking about possibility, we cannot use the negative form of *could.*

  INCORRECT: *I* **could not** *go to the wedding. I'm just not sure yet.*

Maybe or may be

- *Maybe* and *may be* both express possibility, but their forms are different. *Maybe* is an adverb and always comes at the beginning of a sentence. It means perhaps.

  Maybe *he's nervous.*
- *May be* is a modal + verb (*be*). It is always two words.

  He **may be** *nervous.*

A. *Complete the sentences with* may be *or* maybe.

1. _____ he didn't get the invitation.

2. It _____ a long ceremony.

3. It _____ a large wedding.

4. _____ they'll have a big dinner.

5. She _____ wearing a red dress.

6. _____ the wedding will be outside.

B. *Work with a partner. Tony and Angelica are getting married tomorrow. They are worried about everything. One of you is Tony, and the other is Angelica. Think of six possibilities each that can go wrong tomorrow. Use* may, might, *or* could.

EXAMPLE:

A (Angelica): He might get scared and change his mind.

B (Tony): The guests could get lost on their way to the wedding.

PRONUNCIATION

MAYBE AND MAY BE

Maybe is pronounced with stress on the first syllable. *May be* is pronounced with stress on both syllables.

A. *Listen to the sentences. Then listen again and repeat.*

1. <u>May</u>be he's late.
   He <u>may be</u> late.

2. <u>May</u>be she's nervous.
   She <u>may be</u> nervous.

B. *Read the sentences aloud. Stress the underlined words/syllables.*

1. **a.** <u>May</u>be it's a long ceremony.   **b.** It <u>may be</u> a long ceremony.

2. **a.** <u>May</u>be he's at the reception.   **b.** He <u>may be</u> at the reception.

3. **a.** <u>May</u>be it's their tradition.   **b.** It <u>may be</u> their tradition.

CONVERSATION

A. *Listen to the conversation. Then listen again and repeat.*

Kenji: I'm not familiar with your customs. Will you publish your engagement in the newspaper?

(continued)

Heather: No. We've set up our own wedding Web page instead. That's not <u>out of the ordinary</u> today.

Kenji: <u>Now that I think about it</u>, my cousins did that last year. What's on your page?

Heather: My fiancé takes care of the site, but <u>I believe</u> we have pictures and a story about how we met.

Kenji: You should tell that story about how you almost lost your ring.

Heather: <u>Take my word for it</u>, that's not a story I want to broadcast. My fiancé doesn't know about it!

Do you know these expressions? What do you think they mean?

out of the ordinary   now that I think about it   I believe   take my word for it

B. *Work with a partner. Practice a part of the conversation. Replace the underlined words with the words below.*

Kenji: Now that I think about it, my cousins did that last year. What's on your page?

Heather: My fiancé takes care of the site, but <u>I believe</u> we have pictures and a story about how we met.

I think   I'm pretty sure

C. Your Turn. *Write a new conversation. Use some of the words below and your own ideas. Practice the conversation with a partner.*

I believe   now that I think about it   out of the ordinary   take my word for it

Go to page 141 for the Internet Activity.

DID YOU KNOW?	• Guests at a Mexican wedding form a circle in the shape of a heart around the couple. The newlyweds dance within the circle! • In Bermuda, the couple plants a tree during the wedding ceremony. • In Scotland, the groom and most of the male bridal party usually wear kilts.	

A. COMPREHENSION

Circle the letter of the correct answer.

1. Hearst Castle is _____.
   a. an ancient building and gardens that are now used as a zoo
   b. several large, beautiful buildings that a rich American built in the 1900s
   c. the home of a rich Egyptian who brought materials and antiques to America from his native country
   d. a medieval castle that a wealthy European moved from England to California

2. Machu Picchu was _____.
   a. a huge city located by the sea where most Incas lived
   b. a group of caves in the mountains where the Incas hid from the Spanish
   c. a small village built mostly of wood in a valley by a river
   d. a city built of stones on a mountaintop that the Incas used for religious purposes

3. The Chinese Moon Festival _____.
   a. celebrates the beginning of spring
   b. brings families together at harvest time
   c. is a time for worshipping nature and the moon goddess
   d. celebrates the New Year with dancing and singing

4. According to legend, Robin Hood was _____.
   a. a knight who fought alongside King Richard
   b. a dangerous criminal who stole from poor villagers
   c. a thief who fought against evil leaders
   d. a wealthy man who wanted to take King Richard's place on the throne

5. Borobudur is ———.

   a. an ancient temple with Buddhist teachings carved in stone

   b. an ancient stone city where thousands of people lived and worked

   c. a beautiful old building where the British rulers of Java once lived

   d. the ruins of an old castle on a hill that was destroyed by a volcano centuries ago

6. Takada Kenzo _____.

   a. was the first Japanese artist to become famous in Europe

   b. became famous even though his work was very traditional

   c. was a famous painter before he went to Paris to become a fashion designer

   d. introduced new designs and styles to the Paris fashion world

7. Dining customs around the world _____.

   a. don't change much from country to country

   b. are not necessary to know in order to make a good impression

   c. are extremely varied and important for guests to be aware of

   d. are simply a matter of common sense

8. One wedding custom that is similar among most cultures is _____.

   a. using colors and symbols of luck and fidelity

   b. exchanging vows in front of a religious person

   c. having celebrations that last several days

   d. throwing rice to bless the marriage

B. VOCABULARY

Circle the letter of the correct answer.

1. As he traveled, he _____ many beautiful objects to put in his castle back home.

    a. acquired   **b.** designed   **c.** hired   **d.** published

2. Machu Picchu is a(n) _____ sight. It fills you with wonder.

    a. exasperating   **b.** revealing   **c.** astonishing   **d.** conquering

3. She has moon cakes _____ under her arm.

    a. anticipated   **b.** tucked   **c.** captured   **d.** accommodated

4. When King Richard was out of the country, his brother _____ and began to rule the country.

    a. based on   **b.** set off   **c.** longed for   **d.** took over

5. Every year hundreds of people make a _____ to the holy place.

    a. harvest   **b.** pilgrimage   **c.** shrine   **d.** fugitive

6. Nobody knew that the salesperson would _____ as a famous designer.

    a. end up   **b.** long for   **c.** set off   **d.** put together

7. When you are in another country, you can _____ people if you do not respect their culture.

    a. restore   **b.** enforce   **c.** offend   **d.** fast

8. After the wedding, nearly all 500 guests came to the _____.

    a. devotion   **b.** etiquette   **c.** boutique   **d.** reception

C. SENTENCE COMPLETION

Circle the letter of the correct answer.

1. The castle was beautiful, _____?
   a. isn't it   **b.** wasn't it   **c.** didn't it   **d.** wasn't

2. We were _____ to see the temple in such good condition.
   a. surprised   **b.** surprising   **c.** surprise   **d.** surprise by

3. I _____ the Dragon Boat Festival to the Moon Festival.
   a. preferring   **b.** am preferring   **c.** prefer   **d.** prefer than

4. Robin Hood _____ live in Sherwood Forest.
   a. use to   **b.** was used to   **c.** used   **d.** used to

5. Visitors _____ the temple.
   a. are amazed by   **b.** amazed by   **c.** are amazed   **d.** amazed

6. The designer _____ world famous by the time he returned to his native country.
   a. became   **b.** was become   **c.** had become   **d.** is became

7. They give you a bowl of water _____ you can wash your dirty fingers.
   a. that   **b.** that so   **c.** in order so   **d.** so that

8. The wedding _____ in June.
   a. may be   **b.** maybe   **c.** might   **d.** could

WHAT ARE SOME FAMOUS BURIAL TOMBS AROUND THE WORLD?

before you listen

Answer these questions.

1. What famous burial places are there in your country?

2. What kinds of artifacts do archeologists find when they excavate ancient tombs?

3. What have been some of the greatest archeological discoveries in the world?

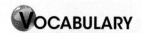

MEANING

🎧 *Listen to the talk. Then write the correct words in the blanks.*

artifacts	defend	legacy	ruthless
currency	excavations	recreate	standardized

1. Some think that the emperor had soldiers put in his tomb to _____ him from armies in the afterlife.

2. The buried sculptures were the artist's _____—a gift to the generations that followed her.

3. When the euro first appeared in Europe in 2002, many people were unhappy about having to give up their old _____.

4. The leader was brutal and unfeeling, so people said he was _____.

5. After Qin Shihuangdi _____ the roads in China, they all had the same width.

6. If we could make things go back to the way they were, we could _____ our childhood.

7. Archeologists find many _____, such as tools and vessels made by humans, during their digs.

8. Archeologists spend many hours digging into the soil during their _____.

WORDS THAT GO TOGETHER

Write the correct words in the blanks.

concerns about	hit upon	life-size

1. I never expected to _____ my grandfather's manuscripts when I went looking through his closet.

2. Because of _____ theft, the archeological site is guarded after dark.

3. This _____ statue is the height of a real person.

USE

Work with a partner to answer the questions. Use complete sentences.

1. What is something you've *hit upon* unexpectedly?

2. What *legacy* has someone famous who has died left behind?

3. Where have archeologists made many *excavations*?

4. What *standardized* tests do students in your country take?

5. Where can we go to see many *artifacts*?

6. How do countries *defend* themselves from enemies?

7. What issue in your country do people have *concerns about*?

8. Why do museums sometimes *recreate* works such as sculptures and put them on display, rather than display the original?

COMPREHENSION: LONG TALK

UNDERSTANDING THE LISTENING

 *Listen to the talk. Then circle the letter of the correct answer.*

1. What is one of Qin Shihuangdi's greatest accomplishments?
   a. He tore down the walls that divided China.
   b. He built many great cities.
   c. He united China under one leader.

2. What was Qin trying to do when he had the terra cotta figures created?
   a. bring his kingdom into the afterlife
   b. fool his enemies
   c. make himself more powerful

3. What makes the terra cotta figures such a great archeological discovery?
   a. their number and size
   b. where they were found
   c. who found them

REMEMBERING DETAILS

*Listen to the talk again. Circle **T** if the sentence is true. Circle **F** if the sentence is false.*

1. In 1974, an archeologist found the first pieces of a terra cotta figure.   T   F

2. The name Qin Shihuangdi means *the First Emperor of Qin*.   T   F

3. Qin had over 4,000 miles of roads constructed.   T   F

(continued)

4. The majority of the tomb is on view, enclosed inside a museum. T   F

5. All of the terra cotta soldiers are wearing the same uniform. T   F

6. Among the terra cotta figures are replicas of musicians and acrobats. T   F

INFERENCE

Circle the letter of the correct answer.

1. From the passage, what can we conclude about Qin's power?
   a. He had limited control over his people.
   b. He was a modest ruler.
   c. He was a ruler of great ambition.

2. What does the terra cotta army tell us about Qin?
   a. He was an art lover.
   b. His people didn't want him to die alone.
   c. His military power was a large part of his identity.

TAKING NOTES: Tombs

Listen and write notes about the description. Which tomb does it describe?

Nefertari's Temple

Taj Mahal

COMPREHENSION: SHORT CONVERSATIONS

Listen to the conversations. Then circle the letter of the correct answer.

CONVERSATION 1

1. What does the professor want the student to do?
   a. write a paper   b. give a talk   c. accept her grade

2. What is the professor's attitude toward the student?
   a. insensitive   b. fair   c. ruthless

CONVERSATION 2

3. Where will the tourist go if he doesn't want to pay more money?
   a. Egypt
   b. Westminster Abbey
   c. Taj Mahal

4. What is the travel agent's reaction to the man's statement?
   a. astonishment
   b. aggravation
   c. depression

CONVERSATION 3

5. Where are the man and woman?
   a. at a restaurant
   b. walking along the street
   c. at a museum

6. How is the woman feeling?
   a. bored
   b. angry
   c. annoyed

ISCUSSION

Discuss the answers to these questions with your classmates.

1. Who was a great leader in your country? What did this leader do that made him or her memorable?

2. Qin Shihuangdi wanted to recreate his empire in the afterlife. If you could go back in time and recreate a time in your life, what would it be and why would you choose it?

3. What legacy would you like to leave to your friends, family, or other people?

CRITICAL THINKING

Work with a partner. Ask each other the following questions. Discuss your answers.

1. Once Qin Shihuangdi had used his army to unite China, he replaced the government with a system run by civilian governors. He built roads and canals and standardized the language and money. Why did these actions make Qin a great leader? What lessons could other conquerors of the time learn from him? What can we learn from him today?

2. Deep respect is one reason why the Chinese have not opened Qin's tomb. Archeologists have opened numerous tombs in Egypt and elsewhere to uncover their treasures and secrets. What are the benefits of excavating ancient tombs? Do you think it's wrong or disrespectful to open these tombs? Do the benefits outweigh the moral concerns? Why or why not?

LANGUAGE FOCUS

MORE RULES FOR THE ARTICLE *THE*

The + noun

- We use *the* with a singular count noun when we talk about something in general. We use *the* especially with names of animals, flowers, and plants.

  The panda is a cute animal.

- We use *the* with the names of inventions and musical instruments.

  *He plays **the** piano.*

The + adjective

- We use *the* before some adjectives such as *old, young, poor, rich,* and *hungry* for a general meaning.

  *The emperor made both **the old** and **the young** work on the roads.*

- We use *the* before nationalities that end in *-ss,-sh, -ch,* or *-ese.*

  ***The** Chinese invented silk.*

  For other nationalities, we use a plural noun ending in *-s* with or without *the.*

  (the) Canadians (the) Germans (the) Americans

A. *Complete the sentences with* the *or with X for no article.*

1. There are problems with _____ rich and _____ poor all around the world.
2. _____ Chinese invented _____ compass.
3. _____ Pekinese is a small _____ Chinese dog.
4. _____ Japanese love _____ sushi.
5. _____ French are known for _____ wine.
6. _____ bicycle is a popular means of _____ travel.

B. *Work with a partner. Ask each other the following questions.*

EXAMPLE:

A: What is your favorite instrument?

B: I like the violin.

- What is your favorite instrument?
- What is the most important invention for you?

- What do you think your government should do for the poor, the young, and the old in your country?
- What are common characteristics of the English, the French, the Chinese, and the Japanese?

PRONUNCIATION

THE SOUNDS *THE* /ðə/ AND *THE* /ði/

The is pronounced *the* (/ ði /) before words beginning with a vowel sound. It is pronounced *the* (/ ðə /) before words beginning with a consonant sound.

A. *Listen to the phrases. Notice the sound of* the. *Then listen again and repeat.*

1. *the* Chinese emperor
   the recent excavations

2. *the* Egyptian pyramids
   the entire army

B. *Listen to the phrases. Check the sound you hear.*

	/ ði /	/ ðə /
1. the tomb	_____	_____
2. the Indian tomb	_____	_____
3. the first emperor	_____	_____
4. the army of soldiers	_____	_____
5. the museum	_____	_____
6. the old people	_____	_____
7. the new invention	_____	_____
8. the gold coins	_____	_____

CONVERSATION

A. *Listen to the conversation. Then listen again and repeat.*

Devin: Did you talk your friends into helping you dig your garden?

Sara: Yes, and <u>little did they know</u> how much work it would be!

Devin: They did a very good job of it, <u>no doubt</u>.

(continued)

Sara: Oh, yes. But we dug out more than dirt, you know. We found old coins and other artifacts!

Devin: You're kidding! Well, <u>obviously</u> it was worth the effort.

Sara: You bet. And <u>thanks to</u> our discovery, I now have people from all across the area wanting to help me!

Do you know these expressions? What do you think they mean?

little did they know   no doubt   obviously   thanks to

B. *Work with a partner. Practice a part of the conversation. Replace the underlined words with the words below.*

Devin: Did you talk your friends into helping you dig your garden?

Sara: Yes, and <u>little did they know</u> how much work it would be!

they had no idea   I didn't tell them

C. Your Turn. *Write a new conversation. Use some of the words below and your own ideas. Practice the conversation with a partner.*

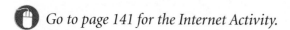

little did they know   no doubt   obviously   thanks to

Go to page 141 for the Internet Activity.

<table>
<tr>
<td>DID YOU KNOW?</td>
<td>

- In Tana Toraja, Indonesia, the graves of royals are represented by wooden dolls placed in balconies on a cliff face. This is called *tau tau*.
- Westminster Abbey in London has the tombs and memorials of Britain's most celebrated scientists, writers, and statesmen such as poet and playwright William Shakespeare, novelist Charles Dickens, physicist and mathematician Sir Isaac Newton, and statesman Sir Winston Churchill.

</td>
</tr>
</table>

WHAT ARE SOME FAMOUS VOLCANOES AROUND THE WORLD?

before you listen

Answer these questions.

1. What are some of the countries with active volcanoes?

2. What causes volcanoes to erupt?

3. What changes on the land take place after an eruption?

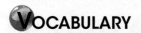

MEANING

Listen to the talk. Then write the correct words in the blanks.

amateur	countless	emerged	intact
constantly	current	erupted	lava

1. I like to read about _____ events because I'm interested in what's happening now.

2. We didn't think the whale would rise up out of the water, but finally it _____.

3. After _____ weeks, the explorers returned and told stories about their many days in the jungle.

4. When the volcano _____ in a violent burst, it sent steam, ash, and hot rocks into the air.

5. _____, or rocks so hot they change into liquid form, began to flow from the volcano.

6. The _____ archeologists are not paid professionals.

7. The earthquake damaged the statue so badly that it's no longer _____.

8. It rained so _____ last month that the sun didn't come out even once in over three weeks.

WORDS THAT GO TOGETHER

Write the correct words in the blanks.

hot temper	put up with	takes up

1. I can't put anything else on my small desk because my computer _____ all the space.

2. Steve has a _____, so we try not to upset him.

3. I can't tolerate this cold weather, so I'm going to Hawaii where I don't have to _____ the snow.

USE

Work with a partner to answer the questions. Use complete sentences.

1. Who do you know with a *hot temper*?
2. What have you done that has taken *countless* hours of your time?
3. What happens to *lava* when it cools?
4. Where do people go when they know a volcano is about to *erupt*?
5. What is an unpleasant situation that you have had to *put up with*?
6. What feature *takes up* the most in your country: mountains, plains, jungles, or water?
7. Which TV program has a contest for *amateur* entertainers?
8. What is something in nature that is *constantly* happening?

COMPREHENSION: LONG TALK

UNDERSTANDING THE LISTENING

Listen to the talk. Then circle the letter of the correct answer.

1. Why is Mark preparing a presentation on the Hawaiian Islands?
   a. His friend told the volcanologists club he would do it.
   b. He is a professional speaker on volcanoes.
   c. He offered to give a talk to amateur volcanologists.

2. How did volcanoes form the Hawaiian Islands?
   a. by causing earthquakes that broke up a land mass
   b. by growing high above the sea floor after many eruptions
   c. by breaking down mountains and sending rocks and earth into the sea

3. According to legend, what did Pele's father do?
   a. sent her away from Tahiti
   b. forced her into the Kilauea volcano
   c. stopped her from fighting with her sister

REMEMBERING DETAILS

🎧 *Listen to the talk again. Circle* **T** *if the sentence is true. Circle* **F** *if the sentence is false.*

1. Mount Vesuvius is located in Italy.   T   F

2. The Big Island has five volcanoes.   T   F

3. Kilauea is the largest active volcano on earth.   T   F

4. Kilauea's lava flows have added 600 acres to the island.   T   F

5. Pele became a goddess after she died.   T   F

6. Legend says that Pele curses anyone who brings rocks to Kilauea.   T   F

INFERENCE

Circle the letter of the correct answer.

1. From the passage, what can we conclude about the Hawaiian Islands?
   a. They will eventually sink back into the sea.
   b. They have not stopped forming.
   c. They are flat islands with few mountains.

2. What can we infer about active volcanoes and earthquakes?
   a. Earthquakes are a warning of an eruption.
   b. Earthquakes always happen after an eruption.
   c. Earthquakes can stop an eruption.

TAKING NOTES: Volcanoes

🎧 *Listen and write notes about the description. Which volcano does it describe?*

Mount Fuji, Japan

Mount Vesuvius, Italy

COMPREHENSION: SHORT CONVERSATIONS

Listen to the conversations. Then circle the letter of the correct answer.

CONVERSATION 1

1. Why does the man want to go into the café?
   - **a.** He's tired of hiking.
   - **b.** He wants to get dry.
   - **c.** He wants to talk to the woman.

2. How is the woman feeling?
   - **a.** irritated
   - **b.** worried
   - **c.** carefree

CONVERSATION 2

3. What is the woman's attitude?
   - **a.** pleased with herself
   - **b.** apologetic
   - **c.** wishful

4. What is the man objecting to?
   - **a.** traveling to six countries
   - **b.** going to Hawaii
   - **c.** carrying things the woman bought

CONVERSATION 3

5. What is the woman's attitude?
   - **a.** amusement
   - **b.** disbelief
   - **c.** sadness

6. What will the man probably do?
   - **a.** refuse the rock
   - **b.** accept the rock
   - **c.** make a joke about rocks

DISCUSSION

Discuss the answers to these questions with your classmates.

1. Would you like to live in Hawaii? Why or why not? What are the advantages? What are the disadvantages?
2. Every year, thousands of tourists go to Kilauea to watch it erupt. Why do people travel so far to see this event? What other places do people go to watch natural phenomena?
3. If you were an environmental scientist, what would you study? Why?

CRITICAL THINKING

Work with a partner. Ask each other the following questions. Discuss your answers.

1. What kind of destruction do volcanoes cause? What other natural dangers are present in other areas where people live? Why do people live near volcanoes and other places where there is possible danger? Should people be stopped from living in certain places? Why or why not?

2. Do you believe that taking rocks from Kilauea will bring bad luck? Why or why not? Are you superstitious? What are some examples of superstitions? Do you believe any of them? Why do you think some people believe in them?

LANGUAGE FOCUS

UNREAL CONDITIONAL IN THE PAST

if Clause			*then* Clause		
Subject	Past Perfect		Subject	*would / could +* Main Verb	
If I	had gone	there last week,	(then) I	would have seen	the eruption.
If the volcano	had been dangerous,		(then) the villagers	would have been warned.	
	hadn't erupted,			wouldn't have died.	

- We use the past unreal to talk about an unreal situation in the past. Both clauses refer to unreal conditions in the past.
- Like other conditional sentences, the *if* clause can come first or second. There is no difference in meaning. If it comes first, there is a comma after it.

A. *Write unreal conditional sentences in the past.*

EXAMPLE:

I took the rock from the volcano. I had many problems later.

  If I hadn't taken that rock, I wouldn't have had all those problems.

1. I didn't take my camera. I didn't have any pictures of the eruption later.

   _____

2. I went to Italy last year. I saw the ruins of Pompeii.

   _____

3. I didn't go to Hawaii last summer. I didn't see the volcano.

   _____

4. You didn't tell me the beach was all black from the lava. I didn't know.

   _____

5. I didn't see it. I didn't believe it.

   _____

6. I bought a travel book. I learned about a lot of unusual sites.

   _____

B. *Do you wish things had been different for you? Write three sentences with the unreal conditional in the past.*

EXAMPLE: *If I had started working when I was sixteen, I could have saved a lot of travel*

money by now.

1. _____
2. _____
3. _____

PRONUNCIATION

CONTRACTION OF *HAVE*

A. *Listen to the sentences. Notice the words that are contracted. Then listen again and repeat.*

If I'd gone, I would've seen it.

If I'd taken my camera, I would've taken pictures.

If I hadn't seen it, I wouldn't've believed it.

B. *Read the sentences aloud. Contract the underlined words.*

1. If <u>I had</u> known the volcano was active, I <u>would have</u> gone to take pictures.
2. It <u>would have</u> been dangerous for you if <u>you had</u> gone.
3. If <u>there had</u> been a danger, they <u>would have</u> given a warning.
4. If you <u>had not</u> told me the mountain was a volcano, I <u>wouldn't have</u> known.
5. If <u>there had</u> been an eruption, it <u>would have</u> been a very small one.

A. *Listen to the conversation. Then listen again and repeat.*

Manfred: <u>Guess what?</u> I'm <u>stuck at home</u> this weekend writing my term paper.

Beate: That's too bad. I'm climbing Mount Saint Helens tomorrow with my hiking club!

Manfred: Really? That's a very high mountain <u>not to mention</u> an active volcano!

Beate: <u>That's right.</u> But we're not planning on going to the top.

Manfred: Didn't they close the mountain because it's too dangerous?

Beate: That was a long time ago. It's currently open. But scientists are watching it carefully.

Do you know these expressions? What do you think they mean?

Guess what?   stuck at home   not to mention   That's right.

B. *Work with a partner. Practice a part of the conversation. Replace the underlined words with the words below.*

Manfred: Really? That's a very high mountain <u>not to mention</u> an active volcano!

Beate: That's right. But we're not planning on going to the top.

and I don't need to tell you that it's   as well as

C. Your Turn. *Write a new conversation. Use some of the words below and your own ideas. Practice the conversation with a partner.*

Guess what?   stuck at home   not to mention   That's right.

Go to page 142 for the Internet Activity.

DID YOU KNOW?

- The three countries with the most volcanoes are Indonesia, Japan, and the United States, in that order.
- There are about 1,500 active volcanoes on Earth today.
- The tallest volcano is Mauna Kea on the island of Hawaii. It is 13,796 feet (4,205 meters) tall.

WHO ARE SOME FAMOUS PEOPLE FROM THE RENAISSANCE?

before you listen

Answer these questions.

1. What is the Renaissance best known for?
2. Who are some famous people of the Renaissance?
3. What do you know about Leonardo da Vinci?

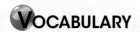

VOCABULARY

MEANING

 Listen to the talk. Then write the correct words in the blanks.

apprentice	diverse	sketched	theory
contemplating	manuscripts	swore	weapons

1. The architect has _____ the first drawings of the building she's designing.

2. The carpenter has a(n) _____ who is learning the trade from him.

3. The researchers found _____ of the author's writings that no one had ever seen before.

4. I'm _____ several different careers but will probably end up choosing engineering.

5. With his hand on his heart, he _____ to his parents that he'd study harder.

6. At the military museum, we saw old _____ once used by the soldiers at the Battle of the Pyramids.

7. During the Renaissance, Copernicus developed an idea, or _____, that Earth revolved around the sun.

8. People of many different ages, colors, and nationalities attended the concert, so it was a(n) _____ audience.

WORDS THAT GO TOGETHER

Write the correct words in the blanks.

a handful of	beyond a doubt	thought up

1. _____ soldiers—five at the most—could fit inside the armored vehicle.

2. While on a quiet walk, the sculptor _____ a perfect design for the statue.

3. The musician's new album was, _____, her best yet, of that the critics were certain.

USE

Work with a partner to answer the questions. Use complete sentences.

1. What does a witness in court *swear* to do?

2. Whose *apprentice* would you like to be?

3. Who uses *weapons* besides soldiers?

4. Where can people find a *diverse* collection of art?

5. Where is a good place to go to *contemplate* something?

6. Who are *a handful of* the greatest artists of all time?

7. What materials can you use to *sketch* a picture with?

8. Who has *thought up* a great invention in modern times?

COMPREHENSION: LONG TALK

UNDERSTANDING THE LISTENING

Listen to the talk. Then circle the letter of the correct answer.

1. What did the duke of Milan find out about Leonardo da Vinci?
   a. that he couldn't paint well
   b. that he had more talents than painting
   c. that he was a better artist than the duke was

2. Why was Leonardo da Vinci considered a man before his time?
   a. He was left-handed and hated war.
   b. He was a great engineer.
   c. He had ideas about things that weren't developed yet.

3. Why didn't Leonardo finish many of his works?
   a. He had too many interests at once.
   b. Too many people wanted him to work for them.
   c. He spent too much time studying one thing.

REMEMBERING DETAILS

Listen to the talk again. Then circle the letter of the correct answer.

1. Who did Leonardo become an apprentice for?
   a. an architect   b. a scientist   c. an artist

2. What did Leonardo do for the duke of Milan besides painting and sculpting?
   a. He worked as a   b. He worked as a   c. He worked as a
   teacher.   soldier.   designer.

(continued)

3. What did Leonardo fail to do with his ideas for inventions?

   a. He never published them.

   b. He never drew up plans for them.

   c. He never sketched pictures of them.

4. How many great works did Leonardo complete?

   a. seventeen

   b. six

   c. forty

5. Why are Leonardo's manuscripts difficult to read?

   a. He used a special kind of ink.

   b. He wrote his words from left to right.

   c. He used unusual words and letters.

6. How was Leonardo different from other Italians of his time?

   a. He put animals in cages.

   b. He painted with his left hand.

   c. He drew self-portraits.

INFERENCE

*Write **F** if the sentence is a fact stated in the talk. Write **I** if the sentence can be inferred from the talk.*

1. _____ Leonardo's teacher promised never to paint again.

2. _____ Leonardo worked for the duke of Milan for seventeen years.

3. _____ During his life, Leonardo's ideas for inventions never became reality.

4. _____ Leonardo wasn't interested in gaining fame or fortune from his ideas.

5. _____ If Leonardo had concentrated on painting, he would have left more finished works behind.

6. _____ Some people think the *Mona Lisa* is a self-portrait of Leonardo.

TAKING NOTES: ARTISTS

Listen and write notes about the description. Which Renaissance artist does it describe?

sculpture by Michelangelo

painting by Raphael

COMPREHENSION: SHORT CONVERSATIONS

🎧 *Listen to the conversations. Then circle the letter of the correct answer.*

CONVERSATION 1

1. What is the mother's tone of voice?

    a. doubtful   **b.** annoyed   **c.** surprised

2. When will the daughter finish her term paper?

    a. before she goes to the museum   **b.** after she visits the museum   **c.** this morning

CONVERSATION 2

3. What class is the woman taking?

    a. pottery   **b.** painting   **c.** sculpture

4. How is the woman feeling?

    a. disappointed   **b.** pleased   **c.** exasperated

CONVERSATION 3

5. What is the father's attitude?

    a. angry   **b.** confused   **c.** thankful

6. Why did the son leave his apprenticeship?

    a. He was working too many hours.   **b.** The job was more difficult than he'd expected.   **c.** He wasn't getting the training he wanted.

DISCUSSION

Discuss the answers to these questions with your classmates.

1. Who is a great artist of the past in your country? What great works is he or she famous for?

2. What does it mean to be ahead of one's time? Who are some people in history who have been ahead of their time? What contribution do such people make to humanity?

(continued)

3. Leonardo da Vinci was different from other Italians of his time. What kind of problems might this have caused for him? Do you prefer to be different from others or to be the same? Why?

CRITICAL THINKING

Work with a partner. Ask each other the following questions. Discuss your answers.

1. What does the word "renaissance" mean? In what ways was the Renaissance a great period in the history of humanity? How would you describe the period in which we are living now? What is great about it? What is not so good? How would you like to see the world change in the future?

2. What does the term "Renaissance man" mean? Which is better, to know a lot about one thing or a little about many things? What are the advantages and disadvantages of being a "specialist" versus a "dilettante"?

LANGUAGE FOCUS

MUST (NOT) HAVE / CAN'T / COULD (NOT) HAVE

Subject	Modal	*Have*	Past Participle	
I / You / He / She / It / We / They	must (not)	have	been	there.
	can't couldn't			

We use the perfect modal form (see above) of *must* and *can* to make deductions about the past.

- We use *must (not) have* to talk about something in the past that we are pretty sure about.

  *Leonardo da Vinci **must have been** a genius to know about flight so long ago.*
  *He **must not have liked** designing military weapons.*

- We use *can't have* and *couldn't have* to talk about something in the past that we are even more sure about.

  *Leonardo da Vinci **couldn't have seen** an airplane because airplanes weren't invented yet.*

A. *Complete the sentences about life in the fourteenth century in Europe. Use* can't / couldn't have *or* must have *and the past participle form of the verbs.*

1. The Italians had beautiful buildings that still remain today. They _____ (have) great architects and builders.

2. Many people _____ (die) when the deadly plague, known as Black Death, swept through Europe.

3. People without formal education _____ (read) books because books were written in Latin.

4. Life in the thirteenth century _____ (be) easy, but it must have been interesting.

5. Florence _____ (be) the place to go if you were an artist at that time.

6. People _____ (be) sure where they were going because they didn't have good maps at that time.

B. *Work with a partner. Imagine that your teacher has not been in class for three days. This is very unusual. Now your teacher is back and looks perfectly normal. Take turns saying four things that* can't / couldn't have *or* must have *happened.*

EXAMPLE: She couldn't have gone on an Alaskan cruise. She was only gone for three days.

PRONUNCIATION

SHIFTING STRESS ON SUFFIXES

When we add a suffix to the end of a word, sometimes the stress shifts.

A. *Listen to the words. Notice how the stress shifts. Then listen again and repeat.*

1. OBject/obJECtion   2. PERfect/perFECtion

B. *Read the words aloud. Underline where you hear the word stress. Then listen to the words and check your answers.*

1. artist / artistic
2. inform / information
3. pronounce / pronunciation
4. economy / economic
5. prepare / preparation
6. permit (noun) / permission
7. science / scientific
8. educate / education

A. *Listen to the conversation. Then listen again and repeat.*

Nick: Did you see Lee's sketch? It's <u>nothing like</u> his other work.

Ollie: Really? How's this one different?

Nick: <u>For one thing</u>, it's a landscape, and he usually sketches people. And the style's different, too.

Ollie: Maybe he had some time <u>on his hands</u> and wanted to try something new.

Nick: That's a good theory. I'll ask him to <u>say a few words about</u> it in class today.

Ollie: That will be difficult. You see, I heard him say he's leaving for Italy this morning!

Do you know these expressions? What do you think they mean?

> nothing like   for one thing   on his hands   say a few words about

B. *Work with a partner. Practice a part of the conversation. Replace the underlined words with the words below.*

Nick: That's a good theory. I'll ask him to <u>say a few words about</u> it in class today.

Ollie: That will be difficult. You see, I heard him say he's leaving for Italy this morning!

> tell us something about   explain

C. Your Turn. *Write a new conversation. Use some of the words below and your own ideas. Practice the conversation with a partner.*

> for one thing   nothing like   on his hands   say a few words about

Go to page 142 for the Internet Activity.

| DID YOU KNOW? | <ul><li>During the Renaissance, it was popular for great works of art to be painted on walls of wet plaster. These paintings were called frescoes because *fresco* means "fresh," as in fresh, wet plaster.</li><li>Galileo (1564–1642), an Italian astronomer, made telescopes that proved that Earth moved around the sun.</li><li>During the Renaissance, Italy was not one unified country. It consisted of 250 separate states.</li></ul> |  |

WHAT ARE SOME UNUSUAL SPORTS IN THE WORLD?

Answer these questions.

1. What is the most unusual sport you have watched or know about?

2. What do you think the sport of orienteering is?

3. What do you think elephant polo is? Where do you think it's played?

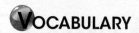

VOCABULARY

MEANING

🎧 *Listen to the talk. Then write the correct words in the blanks.*

| athletic | hilarious | navigate | squash |
| boulder | leisurely | penalty | stream |

1. In football and rugby, the players on the top of the pile _____ the players on the bottom.

2. The situation was so _____ that I fell down laughing.

3. We spent the afternoon walking _____ in the park, relaxed and unhurried.

4. Mark is _____, so he's in good physical condition.

5. Because we used our iPhone for directions instead of just a compass, we received a 20-point _____.

6. A large _____ was in the way, so we climbed over smaller rocks to get around it.

7. After the rainstorm, there was a lot more water in the _____.

8. In the past, sailors had to _____ by using the stars to find their way.

WORDS THAT GO TOGETHER

Write the correct words in the blanks.

| adept at | depending on | figure out |

1. After studying the map for hours, he was finally able to _____ how to get down the mountain safely.

2. Marie is an accomplished athlete who is _____ several sports.

3. _____ the weather, I will either play tennis or video games today.

USE

Work with a partner to answer the questions. Use complete sentences.

1. What sport or skill are you *adept at*?

2. Where might you find a *stream*?

3. Where is there a nice place in your town for a *leisurely* walk?

4. What can happen if you climb on *boulders*?

5. How does a compass help people *navigate*?

6. What show or movie have you seen that had *hilarious* situations?

7. What *penalty* do drivers face when they're caught driving too fast?

8. What physical characteristics does an *athletic* person have?

COMPREHENSION: LONG TALK

UNDERSTANDING THE LISTENING

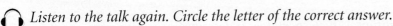 *Listen to the talk. Then circle the letter of the correct answer.*

1. Who can participate in the sport of orienteering?
   a. almost anyone
   b. anyone who is athletic
   c. only serious athletes

2. What do players do during the sport of orienteering?
   a. race together on a single course
   b. find their way from place to place
   c. run along a roadway with markers along the way

3. Why do some people find elephant polo amusing?
   a. Players use a long polo stick.
   b. The elephants do unexpected things.
   c. The players don't know where the goal posts are.

REMEMBERING DETAILS

Listen to the talk again. Circle the letter of the correct answer.

1. Which is true about the woman?
   a. She's not athletic.
   b. She has difficulty finding her way.
   c. She's good at navigating.

2. What does each player get at the start of the race?
   a. a map with places circled on it
   b. directions on how to find each point
   c. a short description of the course

(continued)

3. What is a point?

a. a number given to each player

b. a particular distance covered

c. a certain place on the course

4. At the end of the course, what is each player carrying?

a. a marked card

b. items they had to pick up along the way

c. a walking stick

5. In elephant polo, what determines the length of the polo stick?

a. the height of the player

b. the type of ball used

c. the size of the elephant

6. What happens when an elephant sits in front of the goal post?

a. The player wins the game.

b. The player receives a penalty.

c. The player must get out of the game.

INFERENCE

Write **F** *if the sentence is a fact stated in the talk. Write* **I** *if the sentence can be inferred from the talk.*

1. _____ Orienteering requires a player to navigate from one point to another.

2. _____ There are many different forms of orienteering.

3. _____ At the end of the course, players have proof that they reached all of the points.

4. _____ The man isn't going to try orienteering.

5. _____ In elephant polo, a soccer ball was replaced with a polo ball.

6. _____ The woman doesn't consider elephant polo a sport.

TAKING NOTES: Sports

Listen and write notes about the description. Which sport does it describe?

table tennis (ping-pong)

squash (racquetball)

COMPREHENSION: SHORT CONVERSATIONS

Listen to the conversations. Then circle the letter of the correct answer.

CONVERSATION 1

1. When was the woman at the gym?
   a. at 10:30 A.M.
   b. at 7 A.M.
   c. at 9 A.M.

2. How is the man feeling?
   a. disappointed
   b. aggravated
   c. sorry

CONVERSATION 2

3. What is the coach's tone of voice?
   a. sympathetic
   b. scolding
   c. exhausted

4. Why did the student skip practice?
   a. to study
   b. to play in the band
   c. to play badminton

CONVERSATION 3

5. How is the woman feeling?
   a. disappointed
   b. envious
   c. lucky

6. When will the man go snowboarding?
   a. on Saturday
   b. on Sunday
   c. neither day

DISCUSSION

Discuss the answers to these questions with your classmates.

1. Do you think of yourself as an athletic person? Why or why not? Do sports play an important part in your life? What are the benefits of participating in sports? What are the benefits of regular exercise?

2. Would you like to try orienteering? Why or why not? What are some positive and negative aspects of this sport?

3. Would you like to watch or participate in elephant polo? Why or why not? What are the positive and negative aspects of elephant polo?

CRITICAL THINKING

Work with a partner. Ask each other the following questions. Discuss your answers.

1. Do you like spending time outdoors, or do you prefer indoor activities such as playing computer games or watching TV? What are the advantages of spending time outdoors? Do you think people today spend less time outdoors than previous generations? Do you think they should spend more time outdoors? Why or why not?

2. Are you good at finding your way? Have you ever been lost? What modern devices do we have to help people find their way? Do you think people depend too much on electronic devices rather than using their own instincts, perception, and reasoning? What do you think would happen if all electronic devices suddenly failed?

LANGUAGE FOCUS

GERUND AFTER PREPOSITIONS AND CERTAIN EXPRESSIONS

Preposition + gerund
When a verb is used as a noun and follows a preposition (*about, after, at, before, by, for, from, in, of, on, to,* etc.), it is always in the *-ing* form.

> *I'm looking forward **to snowboarding** this weekend.*
> *I plan **on going** orienteering.*
> *He's good **at playing** badminton.*

Gerund after common expressions
We use a gerund after these common expressions:

> ***be busy*** = *I'm busy **studying** tomorrow.*
> ***can't stand*** = *He can't stand **going** shopping with me.*
> ***have difficulty / trouble*** = *She has difficulty **following** directions.*
> ***It's a waste of time / money*** = *It's a waste of time **going** there now because it's closed.*
> ***It's no use*** = *It's no use **worrying**. There's nothing you can do about it.*
> ***It's not worth*** = *It's not worth **paying** all that money for a ticket when you can see it on TV.*

A. *Complete the sentences with the gerund form of the verbs. Then write two examples of your own.*

1. I'm not really interested in _____ (play) strange sports.
2. I'm fond of _____ (bike).
3. We are looking forward to _____ (go) skiing soon.
4. I don't know what you like about _____ (watch) camels race.
5. He has plans for _____ (go) mountain biking next weekend.

6. It's a waste of time _____ (ask) me to go with you.

7. He's insisting on _____ (take) me to the boxing match.

8. It's no use _____ (try) to make me like it.

9. _____

10. _____

B. *Work with a partner. Take turns telling the things that you are good at, have difficulty doing, and can't stand.*

EXAMPLE: I have difficulty studying when the weather is beautiful outside.

PRONUNCIATION

THE LETTER O

There are many ways to pronounce the letter *o*. One way is as in *snow* (/oʊ/). Another way is as in *love* (/ʌ/).

A. *Listen to the words. Notice the sound of the letter o. Then listen again and repeat.*

1. go   2. mother
   no   some

B. *Listen to the words. Then write them in the correct column.*

polo   come   know   goal   Monday   so   won   grow   does   done   both

/ʌ/ **love**	/oʊ/ **snow**
_____	_____
_____	_____
_____	_____
_____	_____
_____	_____

CONVERSATION

A. *Listen to the conversation. Then listen again and repeat.*

Regina: I'm signing up for soccer this year. <u>How about you?</u>

Peter: Actually, I have plans for playing water polo.

Regina: Are you kidding? Who plays water polo around here? It's <u>a waste of time</u>.

Peter: It is not! I love water polo, and I'm very adept at it. <u>It's no use</u> trying to talk me out of it.

Regina: OK, OK. It's just that I can't stand seeing you miss soccer. <u>You know what I mean?</u>

Peter: I know. But water polo is a new challenge for me. Besides, I love the water!

Do you know these expressions? What do you think they mean?

How about you?   a waste of time   it's no use   You know what I mean?

B. *Work with a partner. Practice a part of the conversation. Replace the underlined words with the words below.*

Regina: OK, OK. It's just that I can't stand seeing you miss soccer. <u>You know what I mean?</u>

Peter: I know. But water polo is a new challenge for me. Besides, I love the water!

I'm sure you understand.   You do understand, don't you?

C. Your Turn. *Write a new conversation. Use some of the words below and your own ideas. Practice the conversation with a partner.*

a waste of time   How about you?   it's no use   You know what I mean?

Go to page 143 for the Internet Activity.

DID YOU KNOW?	• In the Highland Games in Scotland, people toss a tree trunk that measures about 17 feet long. • Three different types of swords are used in the sport of fencing. • Hurling, the national sport of Ireland, is a mixture of hockey, lacrosse, and rugby.	

WHAT IS OCEANIA?

before you listen

Answer these questions.

1. Where is Oceania?

2. What countries are part of Oceania?

3. What islands would you like to visit?

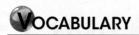

VOCABULARY

MEANING

Listen to the talk. Then write the correct words in the blanks.

characteristics	generations	pristine	staple
comprise	genuine	resort	upbringing

1. My friend is _____, and it's because of his honesty and openness that so many people trust him.

2. The hotel rooms had some unusual _____, including an outdoor shower and lamps made from seashells.

3. The water around the island was pure and unspoiled—absolutely _____.

4. There were three _____ in the photo: his parents, his grandparents, and his great-grandparents.

5. After the child's mother died, an older sister took care of the boy and was basically responsible for the boy's _____.

6. The people used corn in almost all of their dishes, as it was a(n) _____ food in their diet.

7. Most of the books that _____ her collection are travel books.

8. The nice hotel and entertainment made the island _____ a great place to stay while on vacation.

WORDS THAT GO TOGETHER

Write the correct words in the blanks.

get together	laid-back	scented with

1. My friends and I like to _____ on Sundays and just enjoy each other's company.

2. The whole room was _____ the sweet smell of roses.

3. The party will be a relaxed, _____ affair, so you can wear casual clothes.

USE

Work with a partner to answer the questions. Use complete sentences.

1. What family members helped in your *upbringing*?
2. What *characteristics* do you like in a person?
3. Where do you and your friends often *get together*?
4. Where is there a *pristine* area in your country?
5. Would you rather camp on the beach or stay at a *resort*?
6. Who do you know who is *laid-back*?
7. How many *generations* live in your household?
8. What foods *comprise* your list of favorite things to eat?

COMPREHENSION: LONG TALK

UNDERSTANDING THE LISTENING

Listen to the talk. Then circle the letter of the correct answer.

1. What is Oceania?
   a. a small group of islands in the Pacific
   b. a large Pacific region covering most of Australia and a few islands
   c. a vast area of the Pacific containing Australia and numerous islands

2. What are the characteristics of Tahiti?
   a. a warm tropical island with mountains and sandy beaches
   b. a hot desert island with flat land and pristine beaches
   c. a cool, mountainous island with rocky beaches

3. What are important elements of traditional Polynesian life?
   a. modern conveniences and good jobs
   b. large houses with lots of furniture
   c. family, friends, and food

REMEMBERING DETAILS

*Listen to the talk again. Circle **T** if the sentence is true. Circle **F** if the sentence is false.*

1. Micronesia and Polynesia are part of Oceania.   T   F

2. Tahiti is an island in French Melanesia.   T   F

(continued)

3. A traditional Polynesian feast includes singing and dancing. T F

4. Family is a very important part of Polynesian life. T F

5. Corn is a staple food for Polynesians. T F

6. Food is cooked in large pits filled with burning wood. T F

INFERENCE

Circle the the letter of the correct answer.

1. From the conversation, what can we infer about Tahiti?

   a. It's a tranquil and beautiful area to visit.

   b. It's an exciting and busy place to visit.

   c. It's a challenging and difficult place to visit.

2. What can we conclude about traditional Polynesians?

   a. They're serious and hardworking.

   b. They're pleasant but like to keep to themselves.

   c. They're sociable and like to enjoy life.

TAKING NOTES: Islands of Oceania

🎧 *Listen and write notes about the description. Which island does it describe?*

Papua New Guinea

New Zealand

COMPREHENSION: SHORT CONVERSATIONS

Listen to the conversations. Then circle the letter of the correct answer.

CONVERSATION 1

1. Who will the woman tell about the lake?
   - **a.** a government agent
   - **b.** a travel agent
   - **c.** her friends

2. How is the woman feeling?
   - **a.** disappointed
   - **b.** angry
   - **c.** guilty

CONVERSATION 2

3. What is the son's attitude?
   - **a.** anxiety
   - **b.** anticipation
   - **c.** jealousy

4. What food will not be served at the family gathering?
   - **a.** cake
   - **b.** pie
   - **c.** rice

CONVERSATION 3

5. What does the professor want the student to do before school ends?
   - **a.** take a week off
   - **b.** study for her exams
   - **c.** see her friends

6. What is the professor doing?
   - **a.** scolding the student
   - **b.** advising the student
   - **c.** enrolling the student

DISCUSSION

Discuss the answers to these questions with your classmates.

1. Would you like to live on a tropical island? Why or why not? What are the advantages of life on a tropical island? What are the disadvantages?

2. Where would you most like to go on vacation? What is important to you when you're on vacation? For example, do you like to lay back and relax, or do you like to keep active? What activities, if any, do you like to do while on vacation?

3. What foods are most popular in your country and how are they prepared, served, and eaten? Describe a typical gathering of friends and relatives in your culture.

CRITICAL THINKING

Work with a partner. Ask each other the following questions. Discuss your answers.

1. What are some of the characteristics of the people in your country? In general, what are their values? What is most important to them? What are your own values in life? What is important to you?

2. How is tourism a good thing for a country or community? What are the negative aspects? Is your country a tourist destination? How are tourists seen in your country? Have you ever been a tourist in another country? Do people behave differently when they're tourists? How? Why?

LANGUAGE FOCUS

FUTURE TIME CLAUSES

Time Clause		Main Clause	
Conjunction		Simple Present	Future Tense
When	you	go to Samoa,	you will see beautiful beaches.
After	he / she	arrives there,	he / she will enjoy a traditional feast.
As soon as	we	get there,	we will book our hotels.
Before	they	travel to New Zealand,	they will make reservations.

*   We begin a time clause with conjunctions such as *before*, *after*, *as soon as*, or *when*. The simple present is usually used in the time clause. We do not use *will* or *be going to*. Remember: a time clause is a dependent clause and must be used with a main clause.

    CORRECT: *When you get to the island, you **will** see traditional dancing.*
    INCORRECT: *When you get to the island.*

*   We can put the time clause before or after the main clause. When the time clause comes first, we put a comma after it.

    As soon as I get back, I'll tell you all about it.

A. *Complete the sentences with the correct form of the verbs. Add punctuation where necessary.*

1. When I get to Samoa, it _____ (be) nearly midnight.

2. After I get to my hotel I _____ (put) on my summer clothes.

3. As soon as you _____ (get) there you will feel better.

4. They _____ (prepare) a feast for you when you get there.

5. We'll make all our reservations before we _____ (leave).

6. We _____ (call) you as soon as we arrive.

B. *Work with a partner. What will happen in your future? Take turns telling four things that you think will happen. Use time clauses.*

EXAMPLE: When I finish this school, I'll look for a job.

- When . . .
- As soon as . . .
- After . . .
- Before . . .

PRONUNCIATION

HOMOPHONES

Homophones are words with the same sound but different meanings.

> The **weather** is great! I don't know **whether** to go.
> What a **sight**! Have you been to that **site**?

A. *Listen to the sentences. Circle the word you hear. Then listen again and repeat.*

1.	**a.** peace	**b.** piece
2.	**a.** flour	**b.** flower
3.	**a.** seams	**b.** seems
4.	**a.** by	**b.** buy
5.	**a.** scent	**b.** sent
6.	**a.** waist	**b.** waste

B. *Work with a partner. Read the words aloud. Then write homophones for the words.*

1. plane _____

2. two _____

3. week _____

4. beech _____

5. blew _____

6. hour _____

CONVERSATION

A. *Listen to the conversation. Then listen again and repeat.*

Tatjana: Welcome to Adventure Travel. You're obviously here to shop. Tell me what you <u>have in mind</u>.

Rob: Well, I need some hiking boots for sure. I'm going on a walking tour of the Milford Track in New Zealand.

Tatjana: Oh, that's wonderful! The scenery is spectacular there—the mountains, the forests. And the lakes—they're absolutely pristine. You'll have <u>the time of your life</u>.

Rob: I hope so. I'll probably need some sunscreen, right?

Tatjana: Well, <u>I hate to disappoint you, but</u> it actually rains a lot there.

Rob: Oh. <u>I had no idea.</u> OK. Well, as soon as I find some boots, I'll look for a raincoat.

Do you know these expressions? What do you think they mean?

have in mind   the time of your life   I hate to disappoint you, but   I had no idea.

B. *Work with a partner. Practice a part of the conversation. Replace the underlined words with the words below.*

Tatjana: Well, <u>I hate to disappoint you, but</u> it actually rains a lot there.

Rob: Oh. I had no idea. OK. Well, as soon as I find some boots, I'll look for a raincoat.

I don't want to upset you, however   I'm not trying to make you feel bad, but

C. Your Turn. *Write a new conversation. Use some of the words below and your own ideas. Practice the conversation with a partner.*

I had no idea.   I hate to disappoint you, but   have in mind   the time of your life

Go to page 143 for the Internet Activity.

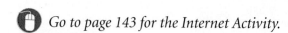

| **DID YOU KNOW?** | • Oceania is made up of sixteen countries.
• The largest country in Oceania is Australia (2,969,907 square miles). The smallest is Nauru (8.1 square miles).
• French artist Paul Gauguin lived in Tahiti and later the Marquesas, both of which inspired his paintings, including the famous *Where Do We Come From? What Are We? Where Are We Going?* which is now at the Boston Museum of Fine Arts. |  |

WHAT ARE SOME SPICES OF THE WORLD?

Answer these questions.

1. Which countries are known for having spicy foods?

2. Why do people from hot climates use a lot of spices?

3. What spices do you use in your country?

VOCABULARY

MEANING

 Listen to the talk. Then write the letter of the correct words in the blanks.

appreciate	curry	milder	spoils
block	enhance	novel	tolerate

1. One dish didn't have as much hot sauce, so it tasted _____.
2. Once food _____, it's unfit to eat.
3. The restaurant's interior design was boring and traditional, but the chef's combination of spices was completely _____.
4. My stomach can't endure spicy foods, but my sister seems to _____ them quite well.
5. The wait staff has been so patient in training me, and I really _____ their help.
6. The farmer put up a fence around her garden to _____ out the rabbits.
7. One simple way to _____ the taste of a food is to salt it.
8. The spicy sauce in this _____ dish makes the vegetables taste good.

WORDS THAT GO TOGETHER

Write the correct words in the blanks.

acquire a taste for	contribute to	make sense

1. It took me a long time to _____ goat's milk, but now I love it.
2. His explanation didn't _____ because I knew he wasn't there when he said he was.
3. He wanted to _____ the effort to feed the poor by helping cook the food.

USE

Work with a partner to answer the questions. Use complete sentences.

1. Which is *milder*: garlic or ginger?
2. How can you show that you *appreciate* something someone has done?
3. What behaviors *contribute to* good health?

4. What kind of foods can't you *tolerate*?

5. What is the most *novel* food you have tried recently?

6. What is something you've *acquired a taste for*?

7. How do you know if a food has *spoiled*?

8. What spices do you like to use to *enhance* the flavor of food?

COMPREHENSION: LONG TALK

UNDERSTANDING THE LISTENING

Listen to the talk. Then circle the letter of the correct answer.

1. Why did ancient people begin to use lots of spices in their food?
   a. They knew that spices killed bacteria.
   b. They didn't get sick when they ate spicy food.
   c. They didn't like the natural taste of food.

2. How do spices preserve food?
   a. They make chemicals that naturally keep food cold.
   b. They produce chemicals that keep food warm and moist.
   c. They have chemicals that prevent bacteria from growing.

3. Why is it good for people to eat spices?
   a. They make food taste more natural.
   b. They cause people to eat food more quickly.
   c. They are healthy for the body.

REMEMBERING DETAILS

Listen to the talk again. Circle the letter of the correct answer.

1. Why did the man complain?
   a. He didn't have enough water.
   b. His curry was too spicy.
   c. His rice was too hot.

2. Why did the man order curry?
   a. He wanted to impress his friend.
   b. He wanted to try something different.
   c. He enjoys eating spicy foods.

(continued)

3. What kind of food do people in Scandinavia eat?

    a. plain food that isn't spiced   **b.** very hot and spicy foods   **c.** food that is mild but spicy

4. Why does the woman mention the Caribbean?

    a. It's hot there.   **b.** The man was born there.   **c.** People eat spicy food there.

5. Which spices were used by ancient civilizations?

    a. onion and cinnamon   **b.** garlic and rice   **c.** tomato and hot peppers

6. Which country is among those that use the most spices in the world?

    a. China   **b.** India   **c.** Serbia

INFERENCE

*Write **F** if the sentence is a fact stated in the talk. Write **I** if the sentence can be inferred from the talk.*

1. _____ If your mouth is hot from eating spices, water only makes it worse.
2. _____ The man didn't understand what he was ordering.
3. _____ If you grow up eating spicy foods you'll probably learn to like it.
4. _____ People in cold climates had a natural advantage over people in hot climates when it came to preserving their food.
5. _____ In countries that use spices, the hotter the weather, the spicier the food.
6. _____ Early explorers tried to find the shortest route to Asia and its spices.

TAKING NOTES: Spices

Listen and write notes about the description. Which spice does it describe?

pepper

saffron

COMPREHENSION: SHORT CONVERSATIONS

🎧 *Listen to the conversations. Then circle the letter of the correct answer.*

CONVERSATION 1

1. What does the man want the woman to do?
   - **a.** clean up at the picnic
   - **b.** cook at the picnic
   - **c.** not come to the picnic

2. What is the woman's reaction?
   - **a.** appreciative
   - **b.** insulted
   - **c.** humored

CONVERSATION 2

3. Who is the woman?
   - **a.** a baker
   - **b.** a police officer
   - **c.** a colleague

4. How does the man feel?
   - **a.** offended
   - **b.** confused
   - **c.** flattered

CONVERSATION 3

5. What is the uncle's tone of voice?
   - **a.** complaining
   - **b.** excited
   - **c.** curious

6. What will the uncle probably eat?
   - **a.** the red curry
   - **b.** the mildly spicy vegetables
   - **c.** the green curry

DISCUSSION

Discuss the answers to these questions with your classmates.

1. Do people in your country cook with a lot of spices? Which spices are popular in your country? Which spices do you use most often in your own food? Which do you like best, spicy or mild foods? What is your favorite dish?

2. Do you like to try new kinds of foods? Have you traveled to places where the food is different from what you are accustomed to eating? What are your favorite foods from other countries? What would you refuse to eat that people from other countries eat?

3. Do you like to cook? Why or why not? Are you a good cook? What do you cook most often? Do you prefer to eat in a restaurant or at home? Why? Do you order take-out food very often? Why or why not?

CRITICAL THINKING

Work with a partner. Ask each other the following questions. Discuss your answers.

1. What kinds of foods did you grow up eating? Do you still like the same kinds of foods? How do you think your childhood eating habits affect you when you are older? What other things in our childhood and upbringing stay with us throughout our lives?

2. How are foods preserved today? Why is there some controversy about preservatives? What are "natural" foods? Why do some people think they're healthier? Do you try to eat "natural" foods? Why or why not?

LANGUAGE FOCUS

VERBS WITH GERUNDS; VERBS WITH INFINITIVES; VERBS WITH GERUNDS OR INFINITIVES

Verbs with gerunds and infinitives follow three possible patterns:

1. **Verb + gerund (base verb + gerund)**
   - We can use the gerund as the object of certain verbs such as these:

consider	finish	keep on	quit	discuss	give up	put off
not mind	dislike	imagine	postpone	stop	enjoy	keep
think about						

   *In the Caribbean, people **enjoy eating** spicy food.*
   - The negative form is **not + -ing**.

   *I **enjoy not cooking** on Saturdays.*
   - We use a gerund after the verb *go* for some activities:

go shopping	go swimming	go camping	go dancing

   *I **go shopping** on Saturdays.*

2. **Verb + infinitive (*to* + base verb)**
   - We use an infinitive after these verbs:

agree	allow	appear	expect	manage	pretend	forget
mean	promise	hope	need	refuse	can't wait	intend
offer	decide	learn	plan	would like	would love	would prefer
want	can't afford					

   *She **refused to eat** the hot curry.*

- The negative form is **not** + infinitive.

  *She **managed not to** eat it.*

3. Verb + gerund or infinitive with no change in meaning
   - With some verbs, such as these, either a gerund or infinitive can be used:

like	hate	can't stand	continue	love	begin	start	try

   *People **started to use** spices in ancient times.* OR
   *People **started using** spices in ancient times.*

A. *Complete the sentences with the gerund or infinitive form of the verbs.*

1. You need _____ (put) salt in it.

2. I tried _____ (eat) the curry, but it was too hot for me.

3. My brother doesn't mind _____ (have) hot food.

4. I was planning _____ (add) some spices to this sauce.

5. I can't afford _____ (buy) saffron, so I'm using an imitation instead.

6. I gave up _____ (eat) spicy foods because I had problems with my stomach.

B. *Make sentences about yourself. Write whether you like or don't like these things.*

EXAMPLE: (cook)   *I love to cook. / I love cooking.*

   - love
   - like / don't like
   - can't stand
   - hate
   - enjoy

1. (eat spicy food) _____

2. (go out to eat) _____

3. (eat sweet foods) _____

4. (go on a diet) _____

5. (go grocery shopping) _____

PRONUNCIATION

EXPRESSING EMOTIONS WITH INTONATION

A. *Listen to the phrases. Notice the tone. Listen again and repeat. Then match the emotions with the phrases.*

Phrases   **Emotions**

_____ 1. Oh, why did we have to come here.   **a.** disbelief

_____ 2. Dinner in four hours!   **b.** excitement

_____ 3. I can't wait!   **c.** regret

_____ 4. I love eating spicy food.   **d.** happiness

_____ 5. This doesn't make sense.   **e.** confusion

B. *How many different ways can you say "Oh, no"? Take turns saying it around the class. Your classmates guess the emotion you are expressing.*

CONVERSATION

A. *Listen to the conversation. Then listen again and repeat.*

Tomas: So, "chef," what are we planning to cook for the big dinner tonight?

Antonio: <u>I don't have a clue.</u> I still need to go grocery shopping.

Tomas: What? Dinner is in four hours! <u>I don't get it.</u> You like to plan these things days in advance.

Antonio: <u>On the contrary!</u> I like to *think* about things in advance, but I prefer *deciding* at the last minute. Then it's a surprise for everyone. Even me! Are you still willing to be my sous chef?

Tomas: <u>Absolutely!</u> Let's start that grocery list.

Do you know these expressions? What do you think they mean?

I don't have a clue.   I don't get it.   On the contrary!   Absolutely!

B. *Work with a partner. Practice a part of the conversation. Replace the underlined words with the words below.*

Tomas: So, "chef," what are we planning to cook for the big dinner tonight?

Antonio: <u>I don't have a clue.</u> I still need to go grocery shopping.

I have no idea.   Who knows?

116 UNIT 14

C. Your Turn. *Write a new conversation. Use some of the words below and your own ideas. Practice the conversation with a partner.*

Absolutely!   I don't get it.   I don't have a clue.   On the contrary!

Go to page 144 for the Internet Activity.

| DID YOU KNOW? | • Saffron is the most expensive spice in the world. About 75,000 saffron crocuses are needed to make one pound of saffron. The threads are picked by hand.
• Ginger is eaten between dishes to clear the mouth. It's believed to help with digestion.
• Cayenne pepper is thought to improve blood circulation. |  |

HOW DOES SCIENCE EXPLORE THE SEA TODAY?

ALVIN

before you listen

Answer these questions.

1. Why have people always wanted to explore the deep sea?

2. Why is it so difficult to explore the deep sea?

3. What is it like in the deepest parts of the ocean?

VOCABULARY

MEANING

Listen to the talk. Then write the correct words in the blanks.

discharge	fluids	illuminate	vents
ecosystem	frigid	thriving	withstand

1. The water was so _____ that the divers needed wetsuits to stay warm.
2. All the plants and animals in an area are part of the _____ there.
3. Lighthouses are built so well that they can _____ even the biggest ocean storms.
4. After it got dark, we had to use the boat's headlights to _____ the surface of the water.
5. Chimneys have _____, or openings, that allow smoke to escape.
6. After you've been seasick, it's good to drink lots of water and other _____.
7. Factories pollute the water when they _____ harmful chemicals into streams and rivers.
8. Outside the area of the oil spill, plants were healthy and _____.

WORDS THAT GO TOGETHER

Write the correct words in the blanks.

forms of	lack of	spewed from

1. The water was very still, and the fish seemed to be suffering from a _____ oxygen.
2. We thought the lake didn't have many kinds of plants and animals, but we saw numerous _____ life on our dive.
3. Water _____ the burst pipe, and got everyone wet.

USE

Work with a partner to answer the questions. Use complete sentences.

1. What country or area has *frigid* temperatures?
2. What is a plant or animal that *thrives* in your country?
3. What are some sources of light that *illuminate* a city at night?

(continued)

4. What are some forces that houses are built to *withstand*?

5. What are some *forms of* life found in the ocean?

6. Why do homes have *vents*?

7. What is an area that has a *lack of* rain?

8. What does a volcano *discharge* when it erupts?

COMPREHENSION: LONG TALK

UNDERSTANDING THE LISTENING

🎧 *Listen to the talk. Then circle the letter of the correct answer.*

1. What is *Alvin*?
   a. a submarine that takes people to the ocean floor
   b. a submersible without scientists that takes equipment into the deep sea
   c. a large ship that scientists use to explore the oceans

2. What are hydrothermal vents?
   a. openings in the ocean floor that let out hot gases from inside the earth
   b. places where the warm Pacific waters and cold Atlantic currents come together
   c. deep canyons formed by undersea volcanoes that have erupted

3. What have scientists found near hydrothermal vents?
   a. areas that are completely barren and lifeless
   b. enormous colonies of common fish and shellfish
   c. strange and previously unknown sea life

REMEMBERING DETAILS

🎧 *Listen to the talk again. Circle* T *if the sentence is true. Circle* F *if the sentence is false.*

1. *Alvin* was the world's first deep-sea submersible.	T	F
2. *Alvin* is capable of staying underwater for ten hours.	T	F
3. Scientists discovered the first hydrothermal vents off the Atlantic coast.	T	F
4. The vents release pure, clear water from deep inside the Earth.	T	F
5. Scientists believed that the ocean floor had an abundance of life.	T	F

6. Near the vents, scientists have found 40-foot squids and ten-legged crabs.   T   F

INFERENCE

Circle the letter of the correct answer.

1. What can we infer about what scientists knew concerning hydrothermal vents before 1977?
   a. They had no idea that they existed.
   b. They could only guess that they existed.
   c. They were certain that they existed.

2. What can we conclude about the new *Alvin*?
   a. It will hold more scientists than the old *Alvin*.
   b. It won't have as many capabilities as the old *Alvin*.
   c. It will allow more extensive exploration than the old *Alvin*.

TAKING NOTES: Sea Life

Listen and write notes about the description. Which sea animal does it describe?

sea urchin

crab

COMPREHENSION: SHORT CONVERSATIONS

Listen to the conversations. Then circle the letter of the correct answer.

CONVERSATION 1

1. Where does the student want to go?
   a. the museum   b. the movies   c. the aquarium

2. How does the roommate feel?
   a. angry   b. frustrated   c. adventurous

(continued)

CONVERSATION 2

3. How is the woman feeling?

   a. slightly confused   **b.** pleasantly surprised   **c.** overwhelmed

4. What does the man think about the woman?

   a. She spends too much time outdoors.   **b.** She should play more video games.   **c.** She stays inside too much.

CONVERSATION 3

5. What are the sisters doing?

   a. swimming   **b.** fishing   **c.** rowing

6. What is Kimberly's tone of voice?

   a. unsympathetic   **b.** understanding   **c.** impatient

DISCUSSION

Discuss the answers to these questions with your classmates.

1. Would you be willing to go down into the sea in a submersible or up into space in a rocket? Why or why not? What characteristics must a person have to do these things?
2. What are the similarities and differences between modern explorers and the early explorers?
3. Why is undersea research important? What can we learn from undersea exploration?

CRITICAL THINKING

Work with a partner. Ask each other the following questions. Discuss your answers.

1. What resources do our oceans provide? What effect is pollution having on our oceans? How does ocean pollution affect humans? If it continues, or gets worse, what problems might arise in the future?
2. What are some of the plants and animals in other ecosystems: desert, river, tropical forest, and mountain? Why is it important to protect these ecosystems? What happens when parts or all of these ecosystems are destroyed by development, pollution, and road building?

LANGUAGE FOCUS

FUTURE PERFECT AND FUTURE PERFECT PROGRESSIVE

Future Perfect

Subject	*will*	*have*	Past Participle	Time Expression
I / You / He / She / It / We / They	will will not (won't)	have	worked	for ten years **by** 2020.

- We use the future perfect to say that an action will be completed before another action or time in the future.
- We use the future perfect with time expressions such as *by the time, by* + time, and *before*.

  By the time you finish your tour, you **will have seen** Alvin.

Future Perfect Progressive

Subject	*will*	*have been*	Verb + *-ing*	Time Expression
I / You / He / She / It / We / They	will will not (won't)	have been	working	for ten years **by** 2020.

- We use this tense to emphasize the continuation of an action up to a certain time in the future. We use time expressions such as *by the time, by* + time, and *before*.

  By the time we finish this tour, we **will have been walking** *for four hours.*

A. *Complete the sentences with the future perfect form of the verbs.*

1. By next year, scientists _____ (find) new species of sea creatures.
2. By next year, they _____ (make) a new submersible that will go deeper than *Alvin*.
3. By 2014, some companies _____ (spend) more money on deep-sea exploration.
4. By 2015, they _____ (discover) new resources at the bottom of the sea.
5. Before 2020, we _____ (build) stations and even small cities under the water.

B. *Work with a partner. Take turns asking these questions and answering with complete sentences. Use* for + *length of time in your answers.*

EXAMPLE:

A: How long will you have been friends with your best friend by the end of the year?

B: I will have been friends with my best friend **for fifteen years** by the end of this year.

1. How long will you have been studying in this class by the end of the year?
2. How long will you have been studying English by the end of the year?
3. How long will you have been attending this school by the end of the year?
4. How long will you have been living in your present home by the end of the year?

PRONUNCIATION

THE SCHWA SOUND: *WAS* / ə /

A. *Listen to these sentences. Notice how the underlined words with* / ə / *are pronounced. Then listen again and repeat.*

It's a great vehicle for scientists to go down to the deep sea.

It was exciting for all of them.

Scientists are finding new forms of bacteria.

B. *Say these sentences aloud and underline the schwa* / ə / *sound. Then listen and check your answers.*

1. More and more scientists are paying attention to this.
2. It took photos for the whole world to see.
3. It was used for the exploration of a shipwreck.
4. It looks at life forms that can survive at the bottom of the sea.

CONVERSATION

A. *Listen to the conversation. Then listen again and repeat.*

Ilhan: By the time we get to the other end, we'll have crawled more than a mile!

Ursula: Wonderful. Thanks to you, I'm crawling around in a frigid cave instead of sitting by the pool.

Ilhan: Don't despair. We're almost there. And you've been doing great until now.

Ursula: You're right. I have to admit, there's an amazing ecosystem in here that I never knew existed.

Ilhan: Yeah, like those bizarre frogs that <u>look like</u> tiny monsters.

Ursula: Hey, you're scaring me. <u>So far</u> nothing has eaten us, but it could still happen!

Do you know these expressions? What do you think they mean?

by the time   Don't despair.   look like   so far

B. *Work with a partner. Practice a part of the conversation. Replace the underlined words with the words below.*

Ilhan: <u>Don't despair.</u> We're almost there. And you've been doing great until now.

Ursula: You're right. I have to admit, there's an amazing ecosystem in here that I never knew existed.

Don't give up.   Cheer up!

C. Your Turn. *Write a new conversation. Use some of the words below and your own ideas. Practice the conversation with a partner.*

by the time   Don't despair.   look like   so far

🖱 *Go to page 144 for the Internet Activity.*

| **DID YOU KNOW?** | • In 1963, the French diver and explorer Jacques Cousteau built a village on the bottom of the Red Sea and lived there with four other divers for a month!
• In 1977, scientists discovered strange chimneys on the bottom of the sea. They called them *hydrothermal vents*.
• The world record for the deepest scuba dive was set in 2005 in the Red Sea by a South African diver who reached 1,044 feet (318 meters). |  |

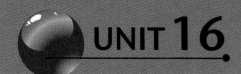

WHO BROUGHT US THE WORLD WIDE WEB?

before

you listen

Answer these questions.

1. What do you use your computer for the most?

2. What type of information do you mostly look for on the World Wide Web?

3. What do search engines allow people to do? Which search engine do you use the most?

VOCABULARY

MEANING

🎧 *Listen to the talk. Then write the correct words in the blanks.*

access	attention	modest	stored
advertisements	diminish	preposterously	trailer

1. I wasn't using my old textbooks, so I _____ them in a box just in case I needed them in the future.

2. The professor was _____ dressed, and no one could believe how absurd he looked.

3. To _____ her colleague's contribution to the project, the researcher lied and said her colleague was lazy and didn't keep good records.

4. No one gave the quiet student any _____, but I knew he was eager to be noticed.

5. The truck was pulling a small _____, which the research assistant slept and ate in for two years before she landed a better paying job.

6. She lost the tickets, but luckily was able to _____ them online and print out replacements.

7. I find pop-up _____ very distracting, but they never persuade me to buy anything.

8. Mark was a(n) _____ student who didn't brag about his academic achievements.

WORDS THAT GO TOGETHER

Write the correct words in the blanks.

keep track of	success story	on campus

1. The account of how Chen achieved his fame is quite a(n) _____.

2. Juanita likes living _____ because she's close to the classrooms and lovely university grounds.

3. One way to _____ your friends' birthdays is to enter the dates in your cell phone.

USE

Work with a partner to answer the questions. Use complete sentences.

1. How does a student get a teacher's *attention*?
2. How do we know when a person is *modest*?
3. Why might someone want to *diminish* the work of another person?
4. Have you used a Web site to *access* someone's biographical information?
5. How do you *keep track of* your appointments?
6. What buildings might you find *on campus*?
7. Whose *success story* would you be interested in learning about?
8. What are some of your favorite TV or online *advertisements*?

COMPREHENSION: LONG TALK

UNDERSTANDING THE LISTENING

Listen to the talk. Then circle the letter of the correct answer.

1. How did Tim Berners-Lee invent the World Wide Web?
   a. He discovered it while doing physics experiments.
   b. He made it while trying to create the first search engine.
   c. He wrote a software program to store laboratory information.

2. How did Larry Page and Sergey Brin create their search engine, Google?
   a. They were experimenting in a friend's garage.
   b. They were working on a school research project.
   c. They were thinking of ways to start their own company.

3. Why did Jerry Yang and David Filo create "Jerry and David's Guide to the World Wide Web"?
   a. They wanted a way to organize their favorite Web sites.
   b. They wanted to get rich and famous by starting their own company.
   c. They wanted to help engineering students with their research.

REMEMBERING DETAILS

Listen to the talk again. Circle the letter of the correct answer.

1. What is the brother's presentation about?
   a. the invention of the computer
   b. the World Wide Web
   c. the invention of search engines

2. Which is true about Tim Berners-Lee?
   a. He's not well known.
   b. He's rich and famous.
   c. He started a billion-dollar corporation.

3. What does the World Wide Web allow people to do?
   a. use information that is stored
   b. search for information
   c. keep track of Web sites

4. What did Berners-Lee make his first real computer from?
   a. cardboard boxes
   b. an old TV
   c. a car engine

5. At what university were Larry Page and Sergey Brin graduate students?
   a. Oxford
   b. Harvard
   c. Stanford

6. Where did Jerry Yang and David Filo live while they were developing their search engine?
   a. in a friend's garage
   b. in a student apartment
   c. in a trailer on college grounds

INFERENCE

*Write **F** if the sentence is a fact stated in the talk. Write **I** if the sentence can be inferred from the talk.*

1. _____ A person's fame does not necessarily indicate the level of his or her accomplishment.

2. _____ Tim Berners-Lee tried to make computers when he was still a child.

3. _____ To develop the World Wide Web, Berners-Lee used a program he had written.

4. _____ Larry Page and Sergey Brin weren't trying to become wealthy when they developed their search engine.

5. _____ Jerry Yang and David Filo were interested in making things easier for themselves when they developed their search engine.

6. _____ Filo and Yang's friends and fellow students quickly started using their "guide."

TAKING NOTES: Computer Pioneers

🎧 *Listen and write notes about the description. Who does it describe?*

Sergey Brin and Larry Page, of Google

Jerry Yang and David Filo, of Yahoo!

COMPREHENSION: SHORT CONVERSATIONS

🎧 *Listen to the conversations. Then circle the letter of the correct answer.*

CONVERSATION 1

1. What *doesn't* the customer need in the device he wants to buy?
   - **a.** a phone
   - **b.** a calendar
   - **c.** games

2. What is the salesperson like?
   - **a.** impolite
   - **b.** helpful
   - **c.** lazy

CONVERSATION 2

3. What is the woman telling the man?
   - **a.** His computer isn't working properly.
   - **b.** It's his fault that he lost his work.
   - **c.** He needs someone else to operate his computer.

4. What is the woman's tone of voice?
   - **a.** scolding
   - **b.** unsympathetic
   - **c.** mocking

CONVERSATION 3

5. How is the student feeling?
   - **a.** amazed
   - **b.** frustrated
   - **c.** resourceful

6. What is the neighbor suggesting to the student?
   - **a.** She should continue searching the Web.
   - **b.** She should look for books on her topic.
   - **c.** She should choose another topic.

DISCUSSION

Discuss the answers to these questions with your classmates.

1. What electronic devices do you own? How much time do you spend every day on your computer, cell phone, and other personal electronic devices? Do you think people spend too much time using their computers and PEDs? Why or why not?

2. How has the World Wide Web made the world smaller? How has it changed customs and cultures? Are these changes always good? Why or why not?

3. Tim Berners-Lee has given his ideas freely and prefers to live a normal life as a professor rather than to seek fame and fortune. What do you think of this? Is his life better or worse because of his decision? Explain. Do you think most people want fame and fortune? Which course would you have taken if you had been Berners-Lee?

CRITICAL THINKING

Work with a partner. Ask each other the following questions. Discuss your answers.

1. How would your life change if you suddenly had no access to electronic devices? How would it affect your work, home life, and social life? Do you think people have become too dependent on electronic devices? Why or why not?

2. What are the positive contributions of the Web? What are the negative aspects of the World Wide Web? What kind of information can people find on the Web that might be dangerous to them or others? Do you think that governments and institutions have a right to censor information on the Web? Explain your answer.

LANGUAGE FOCUS

STATEMENTS IN REPORTED SPEECH

- When we report speech, we usually use *say* or *tell*. We use a pronoun after *tell*. We can leave out *that*.

  *He **said** (that) / **told me** (that) he looked at it.*
- When we use reported speech, we usually move the tense one step back.

Direct speech	Reported speech
He said, "I like it."	He said that he liked it.
He said, "I am considering it."	He said that he was considering it.
He said, "I looked at it."	He said that he had looked at it.

(continued)

He said, "I have tried it."	He said that he had tried it.
He said, "I will buy it."	He said that he would buy it.
He said, "I can do it."	He said he could do it.

A. *Rewrite the sentences as reported speech.*

EXAMPLE:

She said, "I'm selling my laptop computer."
<u>She said she was selling her laptop computer.</u>

1. She said, "Martha can help you." ————————————
2. She said, "Martha knows everything about computers." ————————
3. He said, "I forgot to save his files." ————————————
4. He said, "It will not work on your computer." ————————————
5. He said, "I can search it for you." ————————————
6. He said, "I am working on it." ————————————

B. *Work with a partner. Tell your partner a short sentence. It does not have to be true. Your partner tells the class what you said. Then switch roles.*

EXAMPLE:

A: I have a Web page.

B: My partner told me she had a Web page.

PRONUNCIATION

QUOTING SPEECH

When someone quotes speech, you can hear the quote because the speaker puts a short pause before the words that are quoted. The voice is slightly higher on the quoted words, too.

A. *Listen to the two sentences. Can you hear the quotation marks in the second sentence? Then listen again and repeat.*

She said it's a great search engine. / She said, "It's a great search engine."

B. *Listen to the sentences. Circle the one you hear.*

1. **a.** She said it was a good program. **b.** She said, "It was a good program."
2. **a.** I said it will store it. **b.** I said, "It will store it."
3. **a.** He said don't forget to save your files. **b.** He said, "Don't forget to save your files."

4. **a.** He said we knew all about it.   **b.** He said, "We knew all about it."

5. **a.** She said it really helps.   **b.** She said, "It really helps."

6. **a.** Larry said it's a great idea.   **b.** Larry said, "It's a great idea!"

CONVERSATION

 A. *Listen to the conversation. Then listen again and repeat.*

Erin: Did you hear about the new computer lab? We should <u>take advantage of</u> the new machines.

Keiko: I agree. And someone told me that you can find <u>just about any</u> program you need.

Erin: Wow. Just the idea of it <u>makes my head spin</u>. I think I'll go there after class.

Keiko: But what about basketball practice? You can't let the team down.

Erin: Oh, no. I completely forgot! You know, I can't keep track of all my activities on campus.

Keiko: Yeah, I'm <u>working on</u> that problem myself. Maybe someday we'll have PEDs put directly into our brains!

Do you know these expressions? What do you think they mean?

take advantage of   just about any   makes my head spin   working on

B. *Work with a partner. Practice a part of the conversation. Replace the underlined words with the words below.*

Erin: Did you hear about the new computer lab? We should <u>take advantage of</u> the new machines.

Keiko: I agree. And someone told me that you can find just about any program you need.

make use of   try out

C. Your Turn. *Write a new conversation. Use some of the words below and your own ideas. Practice the conversation with a partner.*

just about any   makes my head spin   taking advantage of   working on

 Go to page 145 for the Internet Activity.

| DID YOU KNOW? | • Ciphers, which are now used to hide credit card details on the Web, were first used 2,000 years ago.
• Science fiction writers such as Arthur C. Clarke predicted today's wired world before the technology existed.
• The Internet came out of a 1969 plan to create a network of computers that would be secure during wartime. |  |

A. COMPREHENSION

Circle the letter of the correct answer.

1. The terra cotta army in China consists of _____.
   a. life-size clay soldiers that are part of the first emperor's tomb
   b. the remains of soldiers who were buried in clay pits in ancient times
   c. the ruins of tiny clay soldiers and weapons the first emperor used to plan battles
   d. ancient drawings and sculptures of the first emperor's actual army

2. The Hawaiian Islands _____.
   a. were formed by volcanoes, none of which are active today
   b. have volcanoes on them that appeared millions of years after the islands formed
   c. are part of a chain of volcanoes that rise from the ocean floor, some of which are still active
   d. were formed when a huge volcano erupted and began sinking into the sea

3. Leonardo da Vinci is one of the greatest men of the Renaissance because he _____.
   a. made great changes in government, science, and society
   b. created hundreds of magnificent paintings during his lifetime
   c. was an accomplished artist as well as an engineer and inventor
   d. wrote brilliant books about war and weapons

4. Orienteering is a sport in which _____.
   a. athletes race against each other on a long track
   b. men on elephants hit a ball across a huge field
   c. climbers race to the top of a mountain
   d. people find their way from one place to another across a large area

5. Traditional Polynesians _____.
   a. have farms and eat a lot of beef and dairy food
   b. enjoy large families and a relaxed way of life
   c. are known for their military interests
   d. live according to strict rules and like to stay to themselves

6. Ancient people learned to use spices in their food because _____.
   a. they discovered that spices prevented food from spoiling
   b. they got tired of eating the same kinds of foods from their region
   c. they knew that spices had powerful chemicals
   d. spices stopped their food from freezing in the winter

7. *Alvin* allows scientists to _____.
   a. get inside of undersea volcanoes
   b. explore areas of the deep sea
   c. travel great distances across the oceans
   d. stay underwater for months at a time

8. The purpose of the World Wide Web is to _____.
   a. put all information on a single computer that everyone can use
   b. help people search for information they need
   c. help people start computer companies of their own
   d. allow people to connect to computers everywhere and use the information available

B. VOCABULARY

Circle the letter of the correct answer.

1. The emperor wanted money to have the same value all over his country, so he standardized the _____.
   a. legacy   **b.** currency   **c.** excavations   **d.** artifacts

2. When they have time away from their regular jobs, _____ volcanologists go inside the craters of volcanoes just for fun.
   a. amateur   **b.** current   **c.** countless   **d.** ruthless

3. We don't know much about some of Leonardo da Vinci's inventions because although he _____ them, he never published them.
   a. swore   **b.** emerged   **c.** sketched   **d.** defended

4. If you do not have a compass, you can use the stars to _____.
   a. erupt   **b.** standardize   **c.** consider   **d.** navigate

5. The air was _____ tropical flowers.
   a. scented with   **b.** put up with   **c.** adept at   **d.** familiar with

6. People use spices to preserve and _____ food.
   a. spoil   **b.** enhance   **c.** appreciate   **d.** tolerate

7. In an area in which we expected to find only one kind of plant, there were numerous _____ fish and sea life.
   a. lack of   **b.** life-size   **c.** forms of   **d.** a handful of

8. Tim Berners-Lee is a _____ man who doesn't brag about his great achievement.
   a. frigid   **b.** pristine   **c.** novel   **d.** modest

C. SENTENCE COMPLETION

Circle the letter of the correct answer.

1. The Chinese invented many things including _____.
   a. the silk   **b.** a silk   **c.** silk   **d.** the silks

2. If you had been here last week, you _____ the volcano erupt.
   a. would have seen   **b.** would see   **c.** have seen   **d.** will have seen

3. Italy _____ the place to be for an artist during the Renaissance.
   a. must be   **b.** had been   **c.** must have been   **d.** must had been

4. He's looking forward _____ next month.
   a. skiing   **b.** to ski   **c.** on skiing   **d.** to skiing

5. When you go to Tahiti, you _____ the beaches.
   a. love   **b.** will love   **c.** will be loved   **d.** to love

6. I expect _____ spicy food when I go to the Caribbean.
   a. to eat   **b.** eating   **c.** to eating   **d.** on eating

7. By 2018, they _____ many more deep sea submersibles.
   a. will built   **b.** will have built   **c.** will have building   **d.** will to build

8. He _____ a Web page.
   a. told that he had   **b.** said he have   **c.** said have   **d.** said that he had

APPENDICES

INTERNET ACTIVITIES

 **UNIT 1**

A. *Work in a small group. Use the Internet to learn more about life in Medieval times. Find the answers to three of these questions. Share your information with your classmates.*

1. How did people spend most of their time?
2. What did they find at their village fairs?
3. Who was educated and what subjects were they taught?
4. What types of clothing were worn by the peasants, nobility, and knights?
5. What types of games did people play?
6. What kind of music was played and on what instruments?
7. What were the customs of marriage and romance?

B. *Use the Internet to find out about one of these fortifications. Find out what the fortification is, who built it, and where, when, and why it was built. Share your information with your classmates.*

The Alamo	Babylon Fortress	Hadrian's Wall	Mannerheim Line
Anastasian Wall	Fort Jesus	Maginot Line	Suomenlinna Fortress

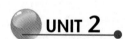 **UNIT 2**

A. *Work in a small group. Use the Internet to learn about Petra. Find the answers to four of these questions. Share your information with your classmates.*

1. Where is Petra located?
2. When was it built?
3. When was it rediscovered?
4. Who rediscovered it?
5. What does Petra mean?
6. Who lived in Petra?
7. What was Petra used for?
8. What remains there today?

B. *Use the Internet to learn about these ancient sites. Find out where each site is located and when it was built. Give a short description of each site. Share your information with your classmates.*

Chichén Itzá	Great Zimbabwe Ruins	The Parthenon
Easter Island	Lascaux	Valley of the Kings

UNIT 3

A. *Work in a small group. Use the Internet to find out about New Year celebrations around the world. Select one of these cultures. Answer the questions below. Share your information with your classmates.*

Armenian	Brazilian	Cambodian	Greek	South Pacific	Thai
Australian	Buddhist	Chinese	Pakistani	Swaziland	

1. When is the holiday is celebrated?
2. What foods are prepared?
3. What is a traditional way in which the New Year is celebrated?

B. *For Hindus, the lotus flower is the symbol of Lakshmi. Flowers and plants have a great symbolic value to cultures around the world. Use the Internet to research the symbolic meaning of one the following flowers and plants. Share your information with your classmates.*

carnation	daisy	iris	lily	sunflower
chrysanthemum	honeysuckle	jasmine	rose	violet

UNIT 4

A. *Work in a small group. Use the Internet to find out about Grimm's Fairy Tales. Choose one of the tales and tell the story to your classmates.*

B. *The earliest known form of Arabic literature is the* qasidah *(ode). Use the Internet to learn about* qasidah. *Find the answers to these questions. Share your information with your classmates.*

1. How many lines are in a *qasidah*?
2. What does this poem usually describe?
3. Into how many parts is the poem divided?
4. What is each part about?

UNIT 5

A. *Use the Internet to learn about one of these UNESCO World Heritage Sites. Answer the questions below. Share your information with your classmates.*

Butrint	Iguazú National Park	Royal Palaces of Abomey
Fatehpur Sikri	Mogao Caves	Tongariro National Park
Great Barrier Reef	Mystras	
Ha Long Bay	M'zab Valley	

1. Where is the site located?
2. What is the site like?
3. Why is it important to the world?

B. *Use the Internet to find out about one of these explorers. Then answer the questions below. Share your story with your classmates.*

Harriet Chalmers Adams	James Cook	Meriwether Lewis
Richard Byrd	William Dampier	David Livingstone

1. When did the explorer live?
2. What famous exploration did the person do?
3. When and where did this happen?
4. What hardships did the explorer experience?

UNIT 6

A. *Work in a small group. Use the Internet to learn about hairstyles in one decade of the twentieth century. Give the name of the hairstyle and describe it. Find pictures if you can. Share your information with your classmates.*

B. *Use the Internet to find traditional clothing and hairstyles in one of these countries. Answer the following questions. Share your information with your classmates.*

Ethiopia	Holland	Iceland	India	Jamaica	Japan	Peru	Samoa

1. What is traditional clothing like in the country?
2. What are traditional hairstyles like?
3. What do these traditions tell us about the people?

UNIT 7

A. *Work in a small group. Use the Internet to find out which came first: the knife or the spoon. What was this utensil first made of? When was it first used? Share your information with your classmates.*

B. *Use the Internet to find a recipe for your favorite meal. Write down the ingredients you need, how to cook them, and how to serve your meal. Share your recipe with your classmates.*

UNIT 8

A. *Work in a small group. Use the Internet to find a traditional wedding custom in one of these countries. Describe what the custom is and what it means. Share your information with your classmates.*

Albania	Egypt	Hungary	Morocco	Russia
Brazil	Fiji	Italy	Norway	

B. *Imagine you are planning a wedding for yourself or someone else. Use the Internet to find tips on planning the perfect wedding. Make a list of ten things to do when planning a wedding. Share your information with your classmates.*

UNIT 9

A. *Work in a small group. Use the Internet to join an archeological dig. Decide what dig you want to participate in and answer these questions. Share the information with your classmates.*

1. What country are you going to?
2. What site are you going to be working at?
3. How long will you be away?
4. What kind of clothes will you wear?
5. What kind of tools will you use?
6. What kinds of jobs might you do?
7. What will you look for?

B. *Use the Internet to learn about ancient Egyptian culture. Answer one of these questions. Share the information with your classmates.*

1. Where did the ancient Egyptians build their homes and what did they use to build them?
2. What rights did Egyptian women have?
3. What trades did boys learn?
4. What foods did Egyptians eat and how were they cooked?
5. What clothing, cosmetics, and hairstyles did they wear?
6. How did they entertain themselves?
7. What did they believe about their pharaohs?

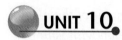 **UNIT 10.**

A. *Work in a small group. Use the Internet to find out about one of these destinations. Find out where the place is located and what there is to see and do. Share your information with your classmates.*

Grand Canyon	Kruger National Park	Nijo Castle	Victoria Falls
Iguazu Falls	Lake Wakatipu	Stonehenge	

B. *Use the Internet to research one of these famous climbers. Find out when and where the person was born and what he or she achieved. Share your information with your classmates.*

Armando Aste	Achille Compagnoni	Reinhold Messner	Ang Rita Sherpa
Una Cameron	John Ewbank	Cathy O'Dowd	

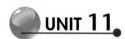 **UNIT 11.**

A. *Work in a small group. Use the Internet to learn about one of these great men of the Renaissance. Find out where and when each man was born and what he accomplished. Share your information with your classmates.*

Filippo Brunelleschi	Albrecht Dürer	William Harvey	Pierre de Ronsard
William Byrd	Lorenzo Ghiberti	Christopher Marlowe	Andreas Vesalius

B. *Use the Internet to learn about one of these explorers. Answer the questions below. Share your stories with your classmates.*

Christopher Columbus	Sir Francis Drake	Ferdinand Magellan
Bartolomeu Dias	Vasco da Gama	Amerigo Vespucci

1. What region did the person explore?
2. When did this happen?
3. Who went with the explorer?
4. What difficulties were encountered?
5. Did the explorer achieve a historical "first"?

 **UNIT 12**

A. *Work in a small group. Use the Internet to find out how, where, and when one of the following sports got started. Share your information with your classmates.*

baseball	luge	snowboarding	windsurfing
basketball	skateboarding	tennis	

B. *Use the Internet to learn about one of these sports figures. Find out where and when each person was born, what sport he or she played (or plays), and what made (or makes) this person famous. Share your information with your classmates.*

Nadia Comaneci	Chen Lu	Michael Phelps
Johan Cruyff	Hideki Matsui	Shaun White
Eddie "The Eagle" Edwards	Yao Ming	
Billie Jean King	Catherine Ndereba	

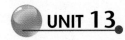 **UNIT 13**

A. *Work in a small group. Use the Internet to learn more about Australia. Find the answers to two of these questions. Share the information with your classmates.*

1. Why is Australia called "The Land Down Under"?
2. What is the "Outback"?
3. What is the size and population of Australia?
4. What is the climate in its various geographic areas?
5. Who were the first people to inhabit Australia and what happened to them?
6. When did Australia become independent from Britain?
7. What are some interesting plant and animal species found there?

B. *Use the Internet to research the lives of the first settlers to Australia OR America. Answer these questions. Share your information with your classmates.*

1. What sort of housing did the settlers have?
2. What was the weather like?
3. What did the settlers eat?
4. How did they get food?
5. Did the settlers have trouble with native people?

UNIT 14.

A. *Work in a small group. Use the Internet to learn about the Chinese Tea Ceremony. Find the answers to one these questions. Share your information with your classmates.*

1. What is the spirit and purpose of the tea ceremony?
2. Where should the ceremony be performed?
3. How should the pots and cups be prepared?
4. How should the tea be prepared, served, and drunk?

B. *Use the Internet to research coffee. Find the answer to one of these questions. Share your information with your classmates.*

1. Where and when was coffee discovered?
2. What is the legend of how coffee was discovered?
3. Where does the word "coffee" come from?
4. Where were coffee beans first roasted and brewed as they are today?
5. When did coffee spread to Europe?
6. What is typical Viennese coffee?
7. What country was the biggest producer of coffee in the nineteenth and twentieth centuries?
8. In what climate and conditions do coffee beans grow best?

UNIT 15.

A. *Work in a small group. Use the Internet to research a remote area. Choose one of the places from the list. Find the answers to the questions below. Share your information with your classmates.*

Amazon Rainforest	Northern Siberia	Sahara Desert	San Blas Islands

1. What is the climate in this area?
2. How many people live there?
3. What group or groups of people live there?
4. What are their traditional foods, clothes, and houses?

B. *Use the Internet to research one of these travelers and explorers. Find the answers to the questions below. Share your information with your classmates.*

James Cook	Mary Kingsley	David Livingstone
Jacques Cousteau	Thomas Edward Lawrence	Beryl Smeeton

1. When and where did the person live?
2. Where did he or she travel?
3. Why is he or she famous?

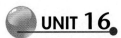 **UNIT 16.**

A. *Work in a small group. Use the Internet to find out about one of these famous names in computer technology. Find out where and when the person lived or lives and why he or she is famous. Share your information with your classmates.*

Paul Allen	Larry Ellison	Jack Kilby
John Backus	Grace Murray Hopper	Pierre Omidyar
Carol Bartz	Steve Jobs	Konrad Zuse

B. *Use the Internet to find definitions for two of the following computer terms. Answer the questions below. Share your information with your classmates.*

boot	cursor	function keys	memory	program
browser	database	hardware	mouse	software
bug	drive	hypertext	network	user
chat	file	language	processor	

1. Do the terms have other meanings that are not related to computer technology?
2. Are there other ways the words can be used? If so, how?

MAP OF THE WORLD

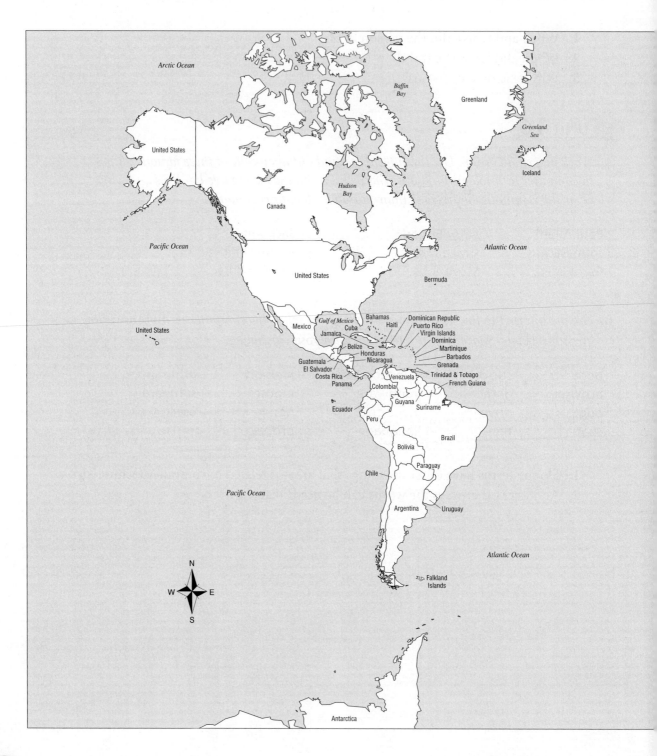

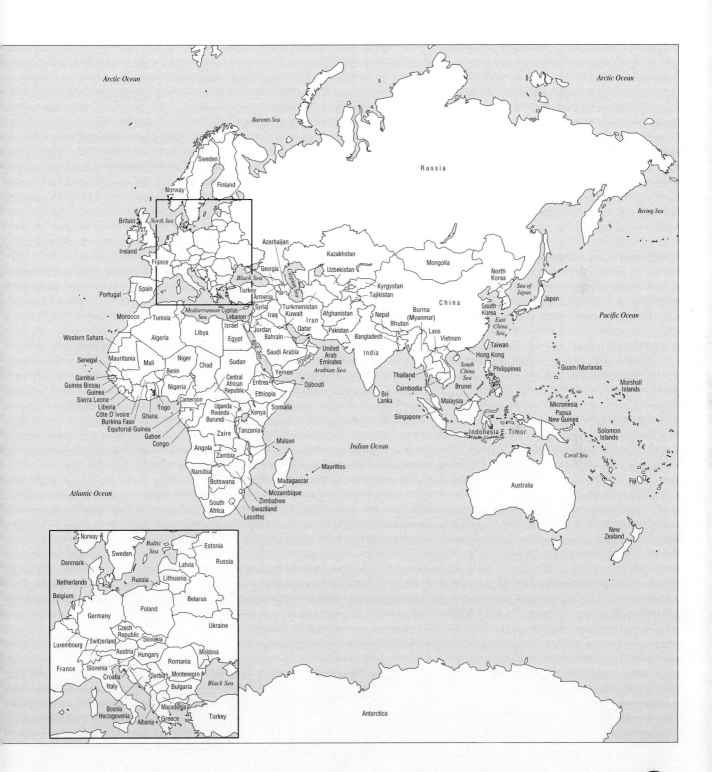

Arctic Ocean

Barents Sea

Sweden

Norway

Finland

Russia

Bering Sea

Britain

North Sea

Ireland

France

Azerbaijan

Kazakhstan

Mongolia

North Korea

Sea of Japan

Japan

Portugal

Spain

Georgia

Caspian Sea

Uzbekistan

Kyrgystan

Tajikistan

China

South Korea

East China Sea

Pacific Ocean

Black Sea

Turkey

Armenia

Morocco

Tunisia

Cyprus

Syria

Lebanon

Iraq

Turkmenistan

Kuwait

Afghanistan

Nepal

Burma (Myanmar)

Laos

Taiwan

Mediterranean Sea

Israel

Iran

Bhutan

Vietnam

Hong Kong

Western Sahara

Algeria

Libya

Egypt

Jordan

Bahrain

Qatar

Pakistan

Bangladesh

Senegal

Mauritania

Mali

Niger

Chad

Sudan

Saudi Arabia

United Arab Emirates

Oman

India

South China Sea

Guam/Marianas

Gambia

Yemen

Marshall Islands

Guinea Bissau

Benin

Arabian Sea

Thailand

Philippines

Guinea

Nigeria

Central African Republic

Eritrea

Djibouti

Cambodia

Brunei

Micronesia

Sierra Leone

Liberia

Côte D´ivoire

Ghana

Togo

Cameroon

Ethiopia

Sri Lanka

Malaysia

Papua New Guinea

Burkina Faso

Uganda

Rwanda

Kenya

Somalia

Singapore

Equitorial Guinea

Gabon

Congo

Burundi

Zaire

Tanzania

Indonesia

E. Timor

Solomon Islands

Malawi

Indian Ocean

Coral Sea

Angola

Zambia

Mauritius

Fiji

Namibia

Madagascar

Atlantic Ocean

Botswana

Mozambique

Australia

South Africa

Zimbabwe

Swaziland

Lesotho

New Zealand

Norway

Baltic Sea

Estonia

Sweden

Russia

Denmark

Latvia

Netherlands

Russia

Lithuania

Belgium

Belarus

Poland

Germany

Ukraine

Luxembourg

Czech Republic

Slovakia

Switzerland

Austria

Hungary

Moldova

France

Slovenia

Romania

Croatia

Serbia

Montenegro

Italy

Bulgaria

Black Sea

Bosnia Herzegovenia

Macedonia

Albania

Greece

Turkey

Antarctica